William Horne

Religious Life and Thought

William Horne

Religious Life and Thought

ISBN/EAN: 9783743423381

Manufactured in Europe, USA, Canada, Australia, Japa

Cover: Foto ©Lupo / pixelio.de

Manufactured and distributed by brebook publishing software (www.brebook.com)

William Horne

Religious Life and Thought

RELIGIOUS LIFE AND THOUGHT.

BY

WILLIAM HORNE, M.A.

MINISTER OF LINDSAY STREET CHURCH, DUNDEE;
EXAMINER IN PHILOSOPHY IN THE UNIVERSITY OF ST. ANDREWS;
AUTHOR OF "REASON AND REVELATION."

WILLIAMS AND NORGATE,
14, HENRIETTA STREET, COVENT GARDEN, LONDON;
AND 20, SOUTH FREDERICK STREET, EDINBURGH.

1880.

LONDON:
PRINTED BY C. GREEN AND SON, 178, STRAND.

PREFACE.

THE following observations on Religious Life and Thought, although appearing in the popular form of Sermons, and printed as they were delivered from week to week to my own Congregation, and having the slightness of structure that such communications require, are not hasty expressions of opinion. They are portions of a deliberately formed body of opinion. The conceptions of religion to be found in them have been elaborated at leisure. The statement of these conceptions is often made with little enough leisure; but I wish it to be distinctly understood that the Sermons do not set forth tentative essays at the solution of a great problem. I would rather that they were looked upon as sundry efforts to familiarize the public mind with results at which I have myself arrived after many years of special study. Not that I suppose for a moment that I have seen wholly round the subject treated of. I know it too well to entertain any such notion. I can honestly make use of words of Kant, applied by him to another subject of inquiry: "Alle Aufgaben auflösen, und alle Fragen beantworten zu wollen, würde eine unverschämte Grosssprecherei, und ein so ausschweifender Eigendünkel sein, dass man dadurch sich so fort um alles zutrauen bringen müsste."

I should like, by these observations, and others that may follow, to contribute towards putting an end both to a narrow piety resting on ignorance of religious history, and sometimes on indifference to it, and to a shallow religious liberalism without earnest religious life. We might have, with our New Testament and nineteenth-century enlightenment to guide us, a religion, rational, serious and humane, in which all good men and women without exception could join, and a science of the greatest human phenomenon, prosecuted by students and experts, who loved nothing so much as truth. But my prompter whispers,

> "Leave the words, sir,
> And leap into the meaning."

BLACKNESS CRESCENT, DUNDEE,
31st March, 1880.

CONTENTS.

SERMON I.
It is expedient for us that one Man should die for the People 1

SERMON II.
A new Commandment 13

SERMON III.
Almost thou persuadest me to be a Christian . . . 25

SERMON IV.
I press toward the Mark 37

SERMON V.
The Captain of Salvation perfected through Sufferings . 49

SERMON VI.
The Common Salvation 62

SERMON VII.
The Spirit of Knowledge 74

SERMON VIII.
The Lord will bring to light the hidden Things of Darkness 86

SERMON IX.
The Spirit of Knowledge (continued) 98

CONTENTS.

SERMON X.
Love worketh no Ill to his Neighbour . . 111

SERMON XI.
That they may be one, even as we are one. . . 123

SERMON XII.
Ye serve the Master, Christ 136

SERMON XIII.
He was wounded for our Transgressions . . . 146

RELIGIOUS LIFE AND THOUGHT.

I.

2ND NOVEMBER, 1879.
Morning Service.

JOHN xi. 49.—"Ye know nothing at all; nor consider that it is expedient for us, that one man should die for the people, and that the whole nation perish not."

IT sometimes happens that a man in speaking a current sentiment expresses more than he is aware of, and touches a truth that his nature is altogether unable to comprehend. That was so with Caiaphas. The notion of substituting one life for another, or for many others, has been a very common one, as you know, and there is nothing in these words of the priest but this idea. There has been a time in the history of every people, or almost every people, when this idea took practical shape, and men and women and children were sacrificed with the express intention of saving others. It was felt to be "expedient," in the words of this Jewish priest, that a human victim should suffer, and that the people as a whole should not perish. To ensure the nation success in war and save it from overthrow and defeat, a man or woman or child was solemnly presented to the god of battle: to deliver them from a threatened plague, a similar offering was thrown to the god who, in the darkness and with hidden and mysterious power, struck down his victims. I shall not take it upon me to recount to you the various occasions in life when this idea was literally carried into effect. But on the erection of a building or a bridge, where we deposit coins and papers and innocent relics, there was laid with due religious ceremony the slaughtered remains of youth and sometimes of beauty: to save, if possible, the king from death, a choice victim was presented to the gods,—the people feeling the expediency of delivering the nation from the universal calamity sometimes attending such an event. The narrative of such things fills us with horror, and we congratulate ourselves that, under the rule of milder manners and more enlightened customs, we have fallen upon the admirable device of substituting coins and newspapers for human life: that when the Queen is ill, we may be asked to offer up prayers, but never to present a youth to the god of disease: that when we go to war—the parallel will not go quite well so far, my friends. It is true we do not slaughter the victim before the battle, but from many of our homes victims are destined to a blood-thirsty and insatiable deity. I said we congratulate ourselves, and I think, on the whole, we have some reason to congratulate ourselves, on the change. I express myself cautiously— perhaps you may suppose with unnecessary caution: but that is a habit which grows upon one, the more one knows of ancient customs, and the better one sees into prevailing manners. The simple outward change seems quite of a revolutionary character, and we suppose, at first, that there can be no question that a great and really solid improvement has taken place along with it. It happens not unfrequently, however, as I have felt many a time, that the inward change is not at all to be measured by the outward. And when you are often surprised by a discovery of this kind, you naturally moderate your tone in considering changes such as I have been mentioning, and feel reluctant to express a deliberate opinion about them. To-day, I am not called upon to give such an opinion; and I would rather direct your attention to the important idea which is, I must own, in a very rude and to us revolting manner, set forth in such practices as I have alluded to. The idea itself, as you are aware, has come to us Christians, by quite a natural descent, in the prevalent notion of the Christian sacrifice, in the substitutionary death of Christ. That is no new idea, nor peculiar to Christianity. In Christianity it took a shape that was slightly different, but it is fundamentally a world-wide conception and of great historical importance. I do not think we do quite wisely or well when we dismiss, as we show great inclination at present to dismiss, these great historical ideas. If you study attentively the various forms they have assumed, and make some effort to get at the truth that was attempted, and sometimes apparently in vain attempted, to be shadowed forth by them, you will look upon them with the greatest reverence and respect. We usually forget in our discussions on such subjects that religious ideas and feelings, like ideas of other kinds, have had a history and a growth and development. It is quite true, and one cannot help being deeply grieved when one considers it—it is quite true that we have been very much in the dark as to this, and that we have been kept in the dark by many whose duty it was to give us enlightenment. The consequence is, that we have regarded all such ideas as in the main stationary, and as certainly very arbitrary. We have taken them up where they were crude and in a very unripe state, and finding them in that condition not precisely what we could wish, we have rejected them, or put them aside as something that we would rather not meddle with. That they are, in certain forms in which we have them, considered revealed truths, and to be simpliciter accepted by us, has not aided us one bit in coming to an intelligent conclusion about them. But, my friends, there is not the very slightest doubt about this point—and I do not give it as an opinion of mine, or a mere opinion of anybody's, but an ascertained truth, and one that you may prove to your own entire satisfaction—that religious ideas and truths, sacrificial and otherwise, have had a gradual unfolding in the course of time, just as other ideas have had. We have no more business to overlook any truth in astronomy, for example, because it had its beginnings in astrology, than we have to overlook and despise a truth in religion because its beginnings lie in a religious condition which may fitly stand to our present state as astrology does to astronomy. The fact being that, if we did all round as we do sometimes, through being wrongly informed, in religion, we should not leave ourselves a leg to stand on. In everything that we at present lean on, there are leaders going into a past with which we may have little or no sympathy, but which has given us all that we now possess. Our notion of a State and the actual State itself, were at the beginning very different from what they are at present. If you had the two placed side by side, you would barely recognize them. But it appears to have been the same with our thoughts and our arrangements as a whole. It cannot be surprising that it should be so with religious ideas and practices. It would be surprising were it not so. When we meet, therefore, with ideas and practices of this kind in far-back times, we are to consider very carefully the times as well as the ideas, and make every allowance for the very gradual progress which thought makes, and especially thought about matters so sacred and so generally revered as religious questions. It is ages before the thought purifies itself from every baser admixture, and comes into the clear consciousness of man as, we may imagine, it exists in the mind of God. Ages, I said; but it may be cycles of ages before dimly-felt and darkly-expressed notions assume shape and proportion, and are assigned their place in the ideal and intellectual world constructed by intelligent souls. Just as creation is not an act once and for all accomplished, by which perfected worlds with their inhabitants are thrown into existence, so neither is the ideal creation performed at a bound. They are both processes. Everything that we see is involved in this process; and as, in the words of a profound spiritual writer, " it doth not yet appear what we shall be," so neither doth it appear what the world shall be—neither what we call the world of mind nor that of matter. But in this long and seemingly slow progress, there is, the past tells us, in religion and other spheres native to man, being evolved a higher and a nobler from a lower and meaner— transformations as wonderful, as beautiful, as unlikely, as from the grub to the butterfly. This view of religion and of thought generally, and of the practices that are built upon both, is inviting and full of instruction. I wish heartily it would dwell more in our minds than it does. If it did so, we should not, when we meet with ideas in the early stages of the process I speak of, reject them as altogether false and erroneous—as having no connection with us. If we knew our own thought aright—and we never can know it without knowing the history of it—if we knew it aright, we should find that it has sprung out of the earlier thought—that, but for this earlier thought, we should not be where we are. It may be a bold thing to kick away the ladder that has helped us to mount to the pinnacle we are on, but we should see always beforehand that there are not thousands and millions struggling on the lower and the lowest rungs. For from the lowest there is a way unto the highest. I said the pinnacle we are on, and it may look high when we gaze beneath us, but it may be, and I believe is, further from the furthest height than we are from the base. The furthest height "doth not yet appear." We are only on an upward flight, if you will allow me to take you with your ladder kicked from under you,—a flight that is never directly up, but slowly ascends by circling swoops that hardly, in their evolutions, seem to come nearer the empyrean at which we only vaguely aim. Ah! my friends, we can all be merry or contemptuous over decaying systems of thought and of belief. If we have any system of thought and of belief at all, just now, it is not to us more stable and true than, what we call, the systems that are doomed and are now passing away. That a similar fate does not await ours, who shall say? If the past is any guide to us, our thought stands equally doomed. For like the sad dethroned gods, who had to give place mournfully to the new rulers in the sky, we feel that "on our heels a fresh perfection treads, born of us and fated to excel us." Then what's the good? you ask; why should we labour to have our labour undone? why think, to have our thought abolished, and knowing that it will be obsolete ere long? why build, that our structure may be overthrown? Partly, my friends, because we must, and cannot help ourselves;

but mainly to prepare for the "fresh perfection." We must, at least, make footprints for her feet, if we do nothing more. She cannot come but on our heels. Why should the sun rise, only to hasten to his certain downfall? Why should flowers bloom, only to fade? Why should we be born, only to die? Why should we build a home and furnish it and tenant it with love, only to desert it in the end? "That," it has been well said, "is the truly permanent and complete which is subservient to a larger scheme and dies into a higher life. The victory which thinkers may win is not that of rounding human thought into a perfect and increscent whole: the crown which they wear is not a garland for their individual brow. Their task is nobler—their reward more blest. To them it is given to be nothing in themselves: to struggle amid darkness and error towards a light firmly believed in, though but dimly seen; to gather up the growing elements of thought at each epoch of man's life, and mould them into forms which shall enable their successors to be wiser than themselves—this is their labour, their reward. Toil unrequited is their glory: failure their success." That is the why of it, my friends, and the reason of a great many things that seem dark as night to us, because we view them as from ourselves, and not from out of ourselves; forgetting that we do not live nor work nor think for ourselves, not even though we are set most resolvedly to do so. We are embraced in a plan whose scope is not open to us. The world is greater than we have conception of. You yourself, my dear friend, are something that you dare hardly imagine. You have never realized what is in your poorest brother and sister. Thought moves on to a point which we cannot forecast. Religion, in belief and practice, has a future before it, which will seem to disjoin it from the present more than the present is from the past, to which I turned your attention, or from any past which I could recal to you. You have heard, I dare say, of an old doctrine, not now much heard of, but which these remarks bring into my mind, and which, although not previously grounded on history and experience, history and experience, from the point of view we are now at, would appear to corroborate. I mean the notion that everything has its type, or pattern, or idea, after which it was made. Plants, animals, the whole structure of the world—man, man's thought and moral action—all had their perfect pattern. In no individual actually existing does the life perfectly agree with the idea of the pattern on which it is modelled. Man is a long way off from the idea of humanity, for example; his moral life is as yet a mere searching out to something far beyond him, but whose existence made this life possible for him; and every step in the direction of moral perfection has, as its ground and reason, this ideal type, however the obstructions in our nature keep us at a distance from it. So that the efforts I mentioned, rude and seemingly ineffectual at first, and entirely rejected by us as we advance, are struggles and inevitable steps to be gone through to reach this ideal, whose existence is only felt as an impulse or instinctive movement in the soul. It is probably this very thought I speak of, that lies at the root of the expression we use very frequently, "Man was made in the image of God." Whereby it is not intended by any means, as is generally supposed, that man was made exactly like God, but that in the formation of man the idea of the divine was the model, type; and towards this type, by gradual ascent and purifying of his nature through generations of effort, the race is finally to win its way. I do not care much whether you carry away such a form of thought with you or not; what I would wish, however, is that, under whatever form you put it, you should clearly see that we are where we are because of what the men and women thought and did before us—that it is mere ignorance in us to despise their thoughts and doings—that our duty is to understand them—to learn what in them—for there is always something in them that is so—to learn what in them is a contribution to the realization of what " doth not yet appear"—faithfully and earnestly to make our contribution, joyfully and wisely vanishing when the fresh perfection is upon our heels.

That may seem to some of you a round-about way of speaking about notions of sacrifice and substitution in religion. But some of you may know in regard to other things, that the round-about way is the nearest road. And it often happens in making for an intellectual position that the same thing is true. Impatient people say, Why not come to the point at once? But there are many reasons for not doing so. Some people would not go one step, if they were taken at once to the spot. And occasionally there are so many obstructions to be removed, that it is a great deal easier to go round than, in the sight of passengers and intending travellers, to remove the obstacles. I have already named to you some forms of the early idea of sacrifice in religion, and which tally very well with the remark of Caiaphas. Among a people in India this very idea was exactly carried out in due form until lately. The victim was made fast to a stake driven into the earth.

The priest, after invoking blessings on the people, that they might have happiness, and prosperity in their cattle, and fertility in their fields, had the man, who was to save the people and ensure them these, sacrificed to their god. And in Africa one tribe has a solemn ceremony, in which a young man is sacrificed in the fields, as they express it, for seed. Kings, out of the same feeling of serving and benefiting the nation, have sacrificed their sons; and the people in great emergency have offered up their ruler. The thought is one familiar and natural in every part of the world where religion has had any hold. We have hints of it in our Bible. Some people think, and it appears to me with very good reason, that the narrative about Abraham offering up Isaac, and then finding a ram and substituting the animal for the man, is a stray record of the transition from human to animal sacrifice. But the entire Jewish ritual is based on the notion of sacrifice, although in this modified form, and in shapes more remote from the earlier practice. And, as I remarked to you, the idea and the thing itself have come to us by right of descent, and Jesus Christ, the crucified, is the centre of the most cultured religion. The idea of Caiaphas has been widened, in keeping with the wider area which the Christian religion occupies, and with the notion of deliverance which it entertains. We do not say that it was necessary that one should die for the nation, and that the whole nation perish not. We say, "Christ died for all," "that the world might be saved through him;" there being in the central doctrine of this religion the most decided conception of sacrifice, and the central figure in it having his place there because of this. It is a great offence to many, that this, what some men call, perfect religion should have borrowed elements belonging to lower and even the lowest phases of religious life. But in saying so, we forget the remarks that I made in bringing you to this point, and to which I would again refer you. There has been no religion without the idea, nor can we conceive one without it. Nay, as we are at present, I cannot conceive life without it. It is a conception that enters into human life, as all true religious ideas do,—there being nothing in them that is arbitrary, unnatural or unreal; but, on the contrary, all that is real, natural and consonant with life. The idea, at first and for a long while perhaps, in the shape and colouring of it, gives us hardly any insight into what it will ultimately unfold itself. But it is at the lowest even, in a stage towards the type and pattern in the heavens that I spoke to you about, the type that we know as love, which seeketh not her own, which, in seeking the things of others, joyfully surrenders self, gives up willingly life, and, what to most people, I think, you will find to be dearer than life, the means to it. I firmly believe that were our town or country canvassed to find men and women who would die to save the people from perishing, a very great many would be ready to do it. Canvass it, my friends, and see how many will sacrifice their standing in society, or incur the risk of placing it in jeopardy; how many will give their time, or surrender their interests, or part with their prejudices, or lose the esteem of their contemporaries, to redeem a manifestly perishing population, and lift it to a life nearer the divine and more resembling the pattern of the human that we know exists. I, for one, would not guarantee that a single person would repay your search. But that is the religious idea of sacrifice which has been purifying itself; and in some shape approaching to that, as our times can furnish it, will this sacrifice on the part of one or more be needed to redeem us from the life we lead. But where to look for it, and how, soberly, to expect it, in days when all sentiment runs counter to the idea that failure is success and unrequited love is glory, baffles us all to say.

II.

2ND NOVEMBER, 1879.
Evening Service.

JOHN xiii. 34.—"A new Commandment I give unto you, that ye love one another."

SURELY, you say, we have heard that before; there is nothing new in it. Christ's ancestors knew something of this, and on an ancient Egyptian scroll some men have deciphered a similar sentiment. Well, I suppose, occasionally expressed sentiments like this, and now and then individual illustrations of them, were not wholly unknown to the world before Christ gave this Commandment. But you are aware of the difference between these two things. Christ does not wish this to have the place of an occasional sentiment with occasional individual illustration. He means it to take its position among the Commandments which have come to be recognized as imperative rules of life—to be recognized and bowed down to, and obeyed as implicitly, and as universally enforced by inward feelings and common opinion, as, say, the Commandments not to kill, not to steal—to be felt as binding upon us as any and all of the great Commandments in the Law—infringement of it, in the least particular, to be followed by remorse as poignant, and by repentance as profound, as murder, theft, adultery. That is more like the position; and if that were not a new thing nineteen hundred years ago, the world was much better then than historians tell us, and a great deal better than it is at the present day. For I see no evidence whatever that this new Commandment is on the same footing as the Ten Commandments. We do not in fact regard it in the sense of a Commandment at all. It is to us something in a great measure optional—a work of, what people long ago called, supererogation. We feel—conscience, men say, tells them—that they must pay heed to the Ten Commandments; but this new one lies outside the sphere of the consciences of us all, and we may, or may not, obey it. If we do so, it will be very gracious on our part; if we do not, we are very "good men of the village" notwithstanding. We need have no feelings such as you describe when we disregard this late addition to the Decalogue; and, in point of fact, we are not conscious of the feelings. We would not tell a falsehood either in plain speaking or in solemn witness-bearing. If we did, we must continually despise ourselves and suffer the keenest reproaches from some internal censor; and if others knew that we had done so, our respect would be gone and our shame insupportable. That is how it stands with the Commandments of the Law.

There is as yet no such visitation on the part of others, nor on our own part, in regard to this new Commandment. We entertain no fear of such a visitation; we should resent it; the whole world at presents resents it. It cannot bear to be reminded that every one is, as a simple duty and command of nature, to love every other. That, you are told, is a matter which must be decided by each man for himself. To be commanded to do it—to base society and public opinion, and form the conscience on such a principle! The thing is a most unwarrantable interference with individual liberty! That, my friends, is perfectly evident. It mightily restricts the kind of liberty you think about and like. But you have not considered what a great blow to this same kind of liberty the promulgation of each of these Ten Commandments once was! You cannot imagine that there was a time when individuals and nations turned round with just such an objection when the prohibitions against stealing and killing and lying were at first issued by some wiser than themselves. Men had been in the habit of now and then abstaining from such acts, but not on commandment, not because they entertained any feeling that it was wrong to do them, not because society would frown upon them for it; but simply because it was their good pleasure to do so. And when it was their good pleasure, without remorse, and without the sting of reproach, they would break one and all of what we now regard as unquestionably first laws of life and plain dictates of conscience. The notion of liberty, at the period of which I am speaking, was precisely this one known to us now, when we hear of prescribing Christian love as a duty. We shall steal if we like, and kill if we like, and have what woman we like, and are strong enough to take and to keep, people said long ago. These are matters that lie wholly within the goodwill of the individual, and are not to be controlled by authority. It is a great breach of the liberty we and our fathers have enjoyed to be obliged to do otherwise, unless we are pleased to do it. That seems to us a very curious state of affairs, and one very difficult perhaps for some of you to believe. But it is good history, and is exactly the position quite commonly taken up with reference to the Commandments of

Jesus. And I have not the slightest doubt in the world that the time will come when our present attitude towards the Christian Commandments, theoretical and practical—practical especially—will be as difficult of comprehension, as the attitude of the people I have described towards universally acknowledged moral truths and laws written on our consciences, as we say. This great Christian Commandment will become in course of time—I speak positively, because society must go in that direction—Christ is the prophecy of what society will be—I say this great Christian Commandment will ultimately become a great moral law, as clear and manifest and indisputable, and as deeply engraved on the tables of men's hearts, as these laws against, what we call, the welfare of the State. At present the position is this—it is written on hardly anybody's conscience—not on anybody's, in the sense in which these other rules are engraved; and it is, at all events, not written on the conscience of society at large. We wonder at the energy and strength of it in Jesus; at the prominence he gave to it in his plan of life; at his calling it a Commandment, and claiming thereby a binding force for it upon all men. The fact is, we do not understand his expression; and we fail to understand it and him also, and fear to go his length, because with him the law was written on his conscience as deeply, nay deeper, than any law in the Decalogue. With us, it is written only in a book; it has not attained the force of inner compulsion, and has not formed round it the awful sanction of mankind. With Christ, it was imperative to love others—as imperative as we feel it to be not to kill any one. With us, it is not so— no more imperative than it was for early peoples to abstain from theft. For the imperativeness is from within. And with these early peoples, as I suggested to you, the inward feeling had not been trained to this. A great authority might inculcate it; but between the inculcation of a wise man and the obedience of humanity from a feeling that their own nature commands it and that the whole world sanctions it, there is an immense and almost immeasurable gulf. There is, on the one hand, a moral chaos, and, on the other, a moral creation; there is a Christ and—well, to say it shortly—Christendom. Some of you may have been interested slightly in the relation sometimes drawn between Christianity and other religions, and their position to each other, so far as regards their moral teaching. There has been a great deal said about these matters, and as the course of inquiry is now setting in, there will be more and more said about them. I would advise any of you who read or hear about such subjects, to distinguish well in your minds, what I have been trying to make out just now, between a floating sentiment, or many such, and the enforcement of a principle as a law of life and a strict commandment of the human conscience—between disjointed sentiments of kindness and goodness to others, and the issuing a commandment from the inner imperativeness of it, with all the sanctions that belong to any commonly and universally acknowledged moral truth. For between these two positions lie, as I need not point out to you, much intervening ground. It is the difference between the man who has heard sentiments about not killing, but who kills if he pleases, and has no feeling of wrong-doing, and the man who, by the powerful inner restraint of feeling, arising in many ways which I shall not stay to describe, and the powerful outward force of opinion, saying, "Thou shalt not," could not, if he pleased; or who, if the united voice of the ages is silenced by some violent, devilish and momentary passion in him, and he does what he pleases, becomes the victim of the furies of an outraged feeling, as we say, really the outraged feeling of the whole world before and after him, which seems to take up its abode in the individual breast. That is the difference between a loose sentiment and a formed commandment, and that, in many cases, on a higher platform of life and thought, you will find to be the difference between Jesus and all preceding teachers in religion, and all succeeding ones, so far as one can see. A difference, you will observe, of degree rather than of kind; but in such degree that it looks absolutely different in kind, and has often misled many into thinking and saying so. But, to return—and I beg of you to note the drift of my remarks, because I consider that there is a very great deal of misunderstanding of Christ, and a wrong opinion entertained about ourselves as Christians, from not attending to the point to which I have been directing you:—you are familiar with me and others saying that we behave unchristianly; that, judged by the Christian religion, which we profess, we are in many things quite irreligious, and, according to Christ, act in a very ungodly manner. You are familiar with this, and some of you, I make no doubt, suppose that it is the getting into a pulpit that inspires such statements; that you might say something to modify them if you had a chance; or perhaps you like to hear them because it is becoming to the occasion. Now I shall say for myself that I would say the same things anywhere, and that it is not mere pulpit eloquence, but statement based on fact and reasons, which no one who looks at Christ and Christendom can well shut his eyes to. I ask you to note the point in the text which I wish clearly to make out to you, and then you can say for yourselves whether I am right or not. I make no mention of the subject of the Commandment of love. You have heard a great deal about it in the course of your lives. I have myself spoken more than once about it to you, and may have occasion many a time again to do the same thing. You know something of what it is, I am persuaded. You may not positively have sat down and drawn out to yourselves all that lies in the phrase, "to love one another as Christ loved;" but in the vague way in which we all may have done this, you can see well enough that Jesus means a course of behaviour very different to what we see about us in the world—very different to what I could point out to you, all over our town and our country. You must acknowledge that. You tell me that it is sentiment—that it is not workable; and you think to shut up all further speech about it. I tell you frankly that we have never tried to work it—not one of us has tried whether it is workable or not. Bring me the man who has, and I shall worship him. I say nothing in the mean time of this love, however. I speak merely of it as a Commandment, as a rule of life, and as placed by Christ on the footing that we put our moral behaviour; and I ask you in all soberness to say if we give this sentiment of love a position as authoritative and binding as we do to respect for property and for life. We do not: the remark I quoted just now, about Christ's teaching being a sentiment, shows we do not. It is like the remark of people in a low stage of life saying that the feeling against murder and stealing is a mere sentiment—not to be thought to be carried out by sane and sensible men—not workable, in fact. And it was not workable with them for many a long day, for the same reason that Christianity is thought not workable now, because they did not try to work on it. It was not workable for the same reason that there are people living in our midst who do not think it practicable to get along if men are strictly to carry out laws against stealing; the impracticability consisting in their not being able to adjust their lives to such injunctions—the inner spirit of their minds rebelling against restraints which are not dictated by their own hearts, or commended, as we say, to their consciences. The culture of this part of their nature, its growth, is, for some reason, far behind the standard that has been all but universally recognized as workable, and to be commanded, and, in fact, insisted on and enforced as alone workable. For, you know, we have come to think quite the opposite of what, we call, lawless and dangerous men think. We have begun to see that society would not hold together long if these commandments were not obeyed voluntarily by the great majority, and if the minority were not, as far as possible, compelled to respect them. So great is the revolution in opinion on what is workable, that what in early times, and by the lawless people among ourselves, is thought pure sentiment and impracticable, is considered by all right-thinking people, as we put it, to be necessary and imperative for the safety of society, and, where the feelings are not perverted, as enjoined by the consciences of all as precepts to be obeyed. It is, then, into this category of precepts to be obeyed, of principles necessary and imperative for the well-being of society, that this injunction of Christ is raised by him. It is no longer a sentiment which you are at liberty to hold or not, which it is all the same whether you carry out or not. It is not in your discretion to say whether it is workable or not. We have all along, as it appears, misunderstood the nature of it. It is a Commandment of life; and, in all full-grown moral life, a dictate of conscience which we can no more attend to or neglect as we please, than we can attend to or neglect as it suits us those Commandments which we should never dream of infringing. You see, my friends, where we are in Christianity. I do not think we have clearly enough seen where we are. We have said to one another: "Oh, if you please, try this Christian scheme of living and loving your neighbour as Jesus did. It is a very noble and elevated idea. It is true perhaps, as you say, that it looks romantic, and there may be some danger of its proving quixotic. I am not sure if you will find it workable. In the experience of Christ it did not certainly appear to work well; but you must feel the admirable character it makes, and there is so much evil that is directly traceable, or which appears to be traceable, to the want of this among us. People are neglected and left to shift for themselves; many, clearly unable to swim, are left to sink; many that might be taught in time to buffet the waters, are abandoned to their own ineffectual attempts; some that might be buoyed up, are frightfully weighted; and we must confess that, were we in their place, we could do no better, and might perhaps do worse. It would be worth while, therefore, throwing in, as an ingredient into the life we lead, a little Christian sentiment. It might ameliorate the frightful state of affairs around us. It is quite true we cannot command you to do it. It is a question of your good-will and good-nature and amiability of heart, and, what some people would call, your general softness of character. It would be pitiful in you to do what we ask you. We can compel you to treat them with proper honesty and humanity, as these are commonly understood. We can exact justice from you. The laws of society and the commandments of the moral law ensure them this at your hands. But we can only beg and entreat you to love them." Such an attitude is wholly unwarrantable. Language like this is not justifiable, and ought not to be used; no more justifiable than it would be to come to an intending murderer and say: "We can use no compulsion nor command; there is no moral prohibition to your act; but it would be pitiful in you were you to desist. There is a law against it, and your own conscience will tell you that you must not eat your victim; but we can only by entreaty and persuasion ask you not to kill."

This Christian Commandment of love is likewise not in your option, and no man is limited to mere persuasion in the matter. It is a question of authoritative and clear command, and not one of good-nature and affability of temper. It is no problem whatever, what effect it would have upon life and trade and society, but a point exactly ascertained; and by the most solemn sanctions that surround any moral law, you are required in your work and behaviour, and general conduct in life and business, to obey this Commandment of Christ's. That is how it stands. That is the meaning of calling this a Commandment. And the active carrying out of this positive effort to do good to the very utmost of our power, and never to do ill to others, is every whit as much a matter of conscience and a part of virtue, as much to be demanded from you, although you have not always been taught so, as your paying your just debts and doing your proper work. Is it to be left to your discretion, my friends, whether, as Christ loved men, you are to do it? It is nothing of the kind. You are commanded to do it. It is one of the Commandments of nature and of God (they coincide when rightly understood) that you should do so. It is no more in your discretion than to commit perjury is in your discretion. Forget for ever the utterly false representation of Christianity and of Christ implied in the sentiments which I gave you an example of just now. It has been to us all a matter of great comfort, and sometimes of congratulation, that such language was held to us—great comfort in this, that if we neglected to do this that our religion enjoins, we had the feeling that we were very "good, careful men of the village" notwithstanding, and not liable to any reproach either from our conscience or from society. We had obeyed all the Commandments of the Law. This other is an ornament of grace, and could by no one be exacted from us. And much congratulation in this, that when we did yield to entreaty and condescended to be gracious, to give more than the Law demanded—when we exhibited to some creature a spark of humanity and love—we had been so benevolent, and, bounding beyond all requirements, done an act that we were not called upon to do. It will be a long time before any men now living make a leap like this, "beyond all requirements." We have not come near to seeing what is demanded from us, and what the duty of life lays upon each of us as a perfectly strict and unavoidable obligation, and no matter at all of "Please you, be kind to the unthankful and the evil;" "If you will be so good, throw love and humanity like Christ's into your business and behaviour, and into your government." We are far, I say, from seeing this as the most solemn Commandment in the Law, and we refuse, absolutely refuse, to make it the basis of life and of society. It lies in our choice, we think. It is in your choice as honesty is. The welfare of society and its progress depend upon it more than upon any other Commandment you can name to me. By the most sacred of sanctions, it is your duty, and not your pleasure—the most sacred of sanctions, I repeat—the conscience of a Jesus and the plain experiences of life.

III.

9TH NOVEMBER, 1879.
Morning Service.

ACTS xxvi. 28.—"Almost thou persuadest me to be a Christian."

WITHOUT the eloquence of a Paul, or of any speaker whatever, and only from the inherent reasonableness of the scheme, and the deepening convictions of thoughtful and serious men, there are not a few among us of the mind of King Agrippa. It is also true, no doubt, if all public channels of information are correct, that there are some who are of a different opinion, and think of renouncing Christianity. But I have not the slightest doubt that were they closely questioned it would be found that it was not Christianity they wished to give up, but their own or somebody else's interpretation of it. These are two very different things, although they are often confounded by hasty and insufficiently informed minds. It is a very sorrowful spectacle, certainly, and the sorrowfulness of it lies in this: that in giving up what is wrong, sometimes the right goes with it; or at least men do not know where to look for the right, or whether there be a right. That there are errors in opinion clustering round Christianity, no man can deny. I am myself always insisting that this is not only the case, but that it must be the case.

For it is with religion as with other things human, that they pass through error, or let me say rather—for it is true to fact—they pass through inadequately apprehended truth to a fuller and fuller comprehension. We have tried, and we have been taught, to regard religion as an exception to everything else with which man has to deal. We have been led to look upon it, and its conceptions and practices, as in some way exempt from the ordinary vicissitudes of human affairs, as raised above the law that appears to be at the root of all life and all thought—the law, I mean, which necessitates everything to pass through stages of growth. We have looked for a perfection in earlier stages in religion, as I had to suggest last Sunday morning,[1] which we do not look for in anything else, and which we had no right to expect in religion. It is part of the error, or inadequate perception of truth, I speak of, that we have ever done this; but it is a very extraordinary and serious blunder to say that because we do not find what we never should have looked for, we give up the whole matter. Religious thought has a history and a growth, even as scientific thought and ideas; and to solemnly abjure religion because in previous times, and lingering into our own times, conceptions prevail which are crude and incorrect, is no more reasonable than it would be for us to give up the quest for knowledge, and the search for everything that comes under the eye of man, because the earliest efforts of this kind were childish and their results erroneous, and because there linger among us, in our speech and practices, relics of these rude efforts of earlier thought. We feel what the proper course is in the search for knowledge. We do not give up seeking; we seek more thoroughly, make more

[1] Sermon I.

exact observations, sift well until we get as near the truth as we can, believing that if this truth is not at once accepted, it finally will be, and that error will die out of itself, or, let me call it, the inadequate truth will die out from sheer inadequacy, or, truer still, will die into a higher life. In the case of knowledge, we do not trouble about it any more than perhaps to note the history of it, or use it as a means of reading the life of men and women that preceded us,—using it as we use old dresses and costumes, quaint and vanished customs, curious dishes and implements, alluvial deposits, anything and everything that can make the past vivid to us, and enable us to see the road our race has traversed, with, as near as may be, the inner and outer details of the travellers' life. To call a halt and say we shall go no further—the people who have brought us here have come a way we cannot go—is a complete misunderstanding of what lies for us to do. We are not called upon to go their way—our duty lies ahead; and the question we have to answer is, at the point you are, how far forward you can march. This, and not to stop and say there has been a series of blunderings, and advance must cease. That is not the way men go to work usually, nor is it the way to go to work in religion. We must advance, if we should blunder still. I don't imagine that we shall be able altogether to avoid blundering for a good while to come; but we must blunder on, my friends, and profit by the blunders. One thing is quite sure: on we must—that cannot cease. The blunders may cease, and will be less and less; but were they greater in number than they are and more serious, that would be no reason for us to give in. I say these things, in passing, with reference to those among us who are persuaded contrarily to Agrippa, who think it their duty to abandon

Christianity. By all means abandon the false in it as you would do the false in everything—the false in thought of all kinds, the false in feeling, the false in trade or in governing, the false in life generally. But you do not give up thinking—you do not drug your feelings—you do not leave business and the duty of governing—you do not throw up life, and would not dream of doing so, because you had resolved to have done with what is untrue and incorrect in them. And why this unreasonableness in the matter of being a Christian? There is this and that which you are convinced is erroneous? Well, my friend, have done with this and that. No one wishes you to cherish error; and religion, above all, counsels you to reject it, and without any glossing whatever, but in the plain and natural and manly sense of the word, to seek the truth and hold to it. And when this and that are away, when everything that is conceivably inadequate has been parted with, is there nothing left—nothing for your own soul to cling to with all its strength—nothing for you to show the world to cling to—nothing at all that you can give as a treasure to the souls that will come after you? Positively nothing? And the whole last nineteen hundred years have, in one circle of human life, and that the innermost and most essential, been spent in hopeless error, and, for that matter, the whole previous existence of man in this sphere has been a dream, a nightmare, and we are only just awaking? This may be so, but it has no counterpart in human experience. Human progress has not been elsewhere a stumbling on through darkness into mere night. Now I do not seek to answer these questions for any one who may be in this mind. If they are to be answered, they must be answered by the persons themselves. They themselves must feel whether, when all that is erroneous is clean thrown away, there is any residue of truth left in our religion, and whether that residue of truth is not, and has not always been, from the time of its Founder and through all that have accepted it, the all-important matter in it.

I think it right to notice this attitude towards religion, chiefly because there is a great deal said about it, and very much also that is not helpful to a real understanding of it. Nor do I imagine that the men themselves who have assumed the attitude, have always a clear knowledge of what they are doing. I am of opinion that if they saw their position in the right light, they would not maintain it as they do: if they ever knew religion correctly, and had a good hold of the history of it and the history of man and of thought, they would not be where they are, nor would they say what they say. But while this class exists and makes its existence known, there is no fear of the world being in ignorance of it, and one great weakness of it is its very loud proclamation of itself and its position: there is a real absence of humility about it, and a very considerable manifestation of vanity. Men go out of their way to let the thing be known—as witness a nobleman in our country telling the public prints that he had renounced Christianity (there is much supposed renouncing of it where it never really has been held or even apprehended): and because the last, and by far the weakest, effort of Strauss was directed against it, as he says; although not in reality against it, but mainly and most strikingly, as I can recollect after seven years, against what I have distinguished, and what everybody but a mere controversialist would distinguish, as the inadequate notions that are joined with it. While this class exists, then, I say, and makes its existence known, we often forget that there is the class to which I alluded at the very beginning of my remarks—men and women who say little or nothing as to their feelings about religion, and whom, therefore, we are very apt to leave out of reckoning in estimating the position of our contemporaries towards Christianity; or, indeed, who may, and sometimas are, reckoned among the class I have been mentioning: men and women of real seriousness of mind and depth of insight into life, and who can take a broad and comprehensive view of man and his nature and destiny. For this modern authority who is accepted as a guide by some and a shaper of their opinions—Strauss I mean—although a man of great ability and fine literary talent and critical skill, wanted many things to make him a competent judge in religion and a true exponent of great religious natures. For, just as there is a faculty in a man which, well cultivated, will give him the right to pronounce an opinion on music, so there is a gift or gifts of the soul which, imparted we know not exactly how, and trained we scarcely know better how, entitle some men to judge in religious events, and to estimate religious ideas. Of course I mean to judge and estimate for others: and Strauss had not the qualities of the latter, although he had many of those of the former. But I was about to remark, that there are in our midst a great many who, from a natural susceptibility to the spiritual side of things which religion keeps before us, feel disposed towards Christianity as this royal personage did—that if our modern nobleman represents, as he says, a great many who do not declare themselves, King Agrippa is also representative of many who are still less likely to declare themselves. Because, for one thing, a native disposition such as theirs, which answers in any, the feeblest, way to what is spiritual, is very shy and retiring. The very uncertainty of their attitude—the "wanting a little of being persuaded"—the force, magnetic-like, turning them that way, but the current not yet powerfully enough felt to make them leap to the loadstone—this uncertainty of attitude, I say, joined to the natural shyness of the temperament, makes this class little known and heard of. But we have them among us, and among us in greater numbers than, from the cries one hears, one would imagine. No speech of man's, as I have said, has brought them to this. If they had listened to the speeches of many good-intentioned, and with no intention, they would have been driven from this. The mere search of their own nature for something to sustain it has led them to the verge on which they find themselves; the growing sense in them that there is a deep natural connection between what is at the heart of Christianity and something which is deepest and strongest in their own heart—the experiences in their own individual lives when they dive beneath the surface-appearances into what is, to most of us, the awful and mysterious profound—the lessons from what is going on around them—the lessons that lie behind them in the great past which is their inheritance—these, when penetrated into—these, repeated and repeated, and pondered over, have reached and aroused feelings in many a soul that no voice of man could move. As you go among men, you will notice in their most earnest purposes, in stray and passing remarks, in obscure and half-concealed feelings, how they stand affected to Christianity, sometimes in actions which they secretly do and are half-ashamed to acknowledge. The indications are not of a kind to be quickly and commonly observed. They can scarcely be discerned and tabulated by men who are after statistics. They are not what we know as "hard and fast enough" to attract attention, were they made duly known to the public. Things now-a-days need to be loudly trumpeted in the ears of men before they will listen. And the one feature of peculiarity about the phase of religious life, or incipient religious life, I speak of is, that it does not call attention to itself by trumpet-blasts, but leaves you to guess at its presence by the most delicate appeals to your observation. It is only through slight hints in the character of the man or woman that they betray their inclination, and the hints are all the slighter sometimes because the men and women are often scrupulously anxious to escape betrayal. Nay, I have found this to be the case—that rather than convey the impression that they had leanings to be Christian, they would attempt to show, and in a boisterous manner, that they leant another way altogether. Their mind is only half made up about it probably. One can see that it is the better half of their mind, however—the hidden and more secret half, where the true man retires to conceal himself from others—the half known only to the possessor, and turned inwards, and only dimly revealed to outsiders—that half of us which sends up the back-thought I spoke of the other Sunday, the thought behind the thought—that half of us, my friends, which makes every one of us either a great deal better than we usually give ourselves out to be, or a great deal worse. For my own part, I think the first is most usually the case. There are exceptions, no doubt; but, as a rule, you will find that if you can get to the inner half of any man or woman, or thing even, you will be at first astonished by discovering how much better they really are than they give themselves out to be. Some of you were never thus astonished? None of us are ever half so often astonished in this way as we should be, because we take no trouble to penetrate to the inner and better half of men and things. We take what we call our first impressions, and form our conclusions from these. But first impressions, even of the open features of a human face, and taken in the most skilful way that art and science can take them, are often curiously untrue. There are men that you do not somehow like; there are opinions that you detest, to use somewhat strong language; there are arrangements and institutions that you cannot help looking upon with great disfavour. Now, in many of these cases, if you went seriously to work, and looked at the inner and the better half, instead of the outer and uglier and worse, you would moderate your feelings towards the men, and your language towards the opinions, and qualify your disfavour of the arrangements and institutions.

It is in this inward part of serious and thoughtful men, then, that you will find the leaning towards what is Christian. But you say, Why does it not come out and declare itself? Why, my friends, does our true self, why does the inward self of everything we see about us, not come forth and manifest itself? I suppose, from some natural delicacy of the inner side of all life—from a dislike to wear, as we say, its heart in its sleeve. We may betray ourselves, as I remarked, in broken hints, in voluntary, and often in involuntary movements, but we do not like to make a full disclosure of the secret man. There are many—I believe there are a great many—who are within a little of being Christian—who, in the part of their nature that I have spoken of, quite recognize the excellence of Christianity, and yield to it—who, when they think with themselves, and in the moments when their hidden half emerges, feel with themselves, that nothing could really be better for them, and nothing better for the world, than their being and the world's being, not almost, but altogether Christians. I dare say we have all had such moments, and that we shall all have them again. People who renounce Christianity, as they say—not knowing very well what they say—because renouncing Christianity means renouncing the civilization of the last nineteen hundred years, and starting in a new line of moral and social life—tearing yourself away from the stream of humanity, and being stranded—there are some things we can do, but some we cannot do — when the Earn has mingled its waters with the Tay, it must onward to the sea—these people also will have such moments as I have spoken of. They cannot very well escape having them, for the power of persuasion on these matters at present does not lie, as it seems to me, in hearing this man or that—a Paul or any one else; the power is working in men's souls; the persuasion appears to come more from within than from without; to be directly and immediately in contact with our inner life, silently but persistently working in the hearts and consciences of the best among us, reaching the inner ear with a power and conviction that no outward appeal can rival. It is the spirit of Christ working in the hearts of our generation—in hearts that have been through long ages now preparing for the inward pressing home of the gospel of love and goodness and peace. And many who say nothing, and who would be the last to send a letter to a newspaper about it, are profoundly affected in the inner side of their nature; earnestly convinced there that what is the inmost matter in Christianity is not a thing to be given up, but to be taken home to the heart and nourished like the dear life. For, corresponding to the double aspect that we present to ourselves, and which you will find in the men about you, there is also an inner and an outer in Christianity—an outer that has repelled some people. There is no denying that it has put on shapes which those who could not get behind the shape found to be very objectionable; which they, foolishly taking these for the whole—inner and outer half as well—have turned away from. But when this side of our own nature is directed, as it appears to me to be at present, to the same side of Christianity, there is produced in all honest natures a strong conviction that, apart altogether from the sacred character of religion—from the peculiar position accorded to Jesus—from the question of the nature of the Bible—entirely putting aside everything as to the source and origin of Christianity—there is a persuasion that its principles claim their recognition; and more than that, they are all but ready to give allegiance to them, and to seek it from others. There are many things taking place around us which seem to contradict what I am saying; but let each of you consider his best acquaintances—take them at their best moments—in the undress of their character—take the uneasy feeling that you find pervading society, and which will hardly take more definite shape than to acknowledge that there must be something wrong somewhere—that our business lacks a somewhat—that our whole relations in society are not as they should be—the sense that something must be done to better the state of matters that surrounds us—that, were it not for this and that obligation, which we have incurred in life, and which we cannot shake off, were it not for the risk of the thing failing, did it not mean braving the opinion of our class and our associates, did it not involve our displaying to the world the inmost and dearest feelings of our heart—the very springs of our soul—we feel constrained to model our lives, the management of our business, the execution of our work, the treatment of our fellow-men, the building-up of our own characters, and the shaping of our children's, on that of Jesus. There is the inward debating going on, and the inclination one has is to hurry the debate to a conclusion. It is a "still-fermenting process," which those who see the end can watch with patience and composure, knowing surely that the new wine of life is there and will gladden men's souls, though they may never live to see it—the inward debating will resolve itself, and the thoughts of men's hearts be revealed, though this revelation come too late for them—the inner will become outer—men will no longer be almost but altogether Christian—there will be not one, but a peopled universe of Christs—new creatures after the type of the first-born—nay, if there was anything in his predictive power, transcending him: "Greater works than these shall ye do." But in what sense greater, I cannot say to-day; nor need we, for many a day, inquire—not, at least, until we have done equal to him, can we speak of doing greater than he did.

IV.

9TH NOVEMBER, 1879.
Evening Service.

PHILIP. iii. 14.—"I press toward the mark for the prize of the high calling of God in Christ Jesus."

YOU hear it said sometimes, and I have felt it myself often, that the ideal set before us in Christianity is a very questionable thing to teach; questionable, of course, in a practical point of view. It is a point of very great nicety, were we to go into the details of such a discussion; but it is broadly stated, and by one who has great right to be heard on such a subject, that the holding up of such a life as the Christian has, instead of benefiting, actually done considerable injury to morality.[1] That, I need not say, has been a long way from the intention of men who have held before others the true pattern of human living as they thought they discerned it in Jesus. Their aim, and the aim, I take it, of all religious teaching, is chiefly to quicken moral feeling and perception, and purify and raise the moral life. So that if there is a better way in which this can be done than the way that we have been in the habit of pursuing, it is the duty of every one to inquire into this way and to follow it. There is nothing gained by our sticking

[1] Spencer's "Data of Ethics."

to a plan or principle, or anything, because we have done so for a long time, and because the great majority of people about us do the same thing. Now as to the moral training of men and women, I am willing to admit that it is not a question that can be settled off-hand and without consideration—that we are to take for granted that we at present know the best possible method, or that, knowing it, we apply it in the best possible way. I think moral teaching—which, as you are aware, I consider the main thing in religion, with my own meaning of what is moral—I think moral teaching a much more difficult and involved matter than that—slightly more serious than Mr. Bright would seem to consider it—containing in it reaches a great deal beyond the inculcation of kindness to dogs and cats and other loveable animals, important as that may be. And the plan to be pursued stands, therefore, to my mind constantly open to revision and possible improvement; and the suggestions of really competent men are to be maturely and carefully considered, and without reference to the quarter where they come from. From whatever quarter of thought, secular or religious, I am very strongly convinced of this, that there is no man of any note or weight in our thinking world but who is really and honestly desirous to see the people improved and elevated morally. There may be differences of standpoint and of method, but there is, I am positive, absolute unity in this desire. Now when I speak of the ideal in Christianity, I have not in my mind the very arbitrary rules sometimes enforced and inculcated, or which, in former days, were enforced by sincere, religious men and women. I do not think of the harsh and repellent aspect that in some cases, under this kind of teaching, was given to religion and morality—of the confusion of " the needless with the needful commands"[1]—of the indiscriminate prohibition of innocent pleasure, and pleasure that might be injurious—of the want of sympathy with nature, and especially with young nature—the entire absence of a broad and healthy and generous view of human life and needs. I have not this in my mind, because, although there may be yet instances here and there of this, that is called occasionally the harsh and severe ethics of the past, I do not imagine that at present we stand in great danger from it. We shall all allow that, with much that was good in this teaching—and a great deal of it has been associated with Scotland, as you know—with the Scottish character and religion—with much that was undeniably good, there was a considerable deal of mischief. I shall not enter into the mischief of it. It gave us, however, very noble characters sometimes—with great strength and much narrowness; and, occasionally, it cannot be questioned, it greatly depreciated morals, and thus presented to us the painful contrast of a rigorous and unbending life with one that was uncommonly the reverse. What is now objected to the Christian morality is not this so much, as what is called the impracticability of its ideal—the setting before men and women, encompassed with all the difficult conditions of living and working, principles of conduct which they feel it beyond them to carry into effect. It is, my friends, a very grave objection, if there is weight in it; it is one, as I said, that strikes many of us, more perhaps in the way of vague feeling than of clearly expressed opinion. I shall put it to you in the words of one who treats it more as an intellectual opinion than as a feeling, and who expresses and maintains the objection with a clearness that leaves nothing

[1] Spencer.

to be desired. For next to knowing your own position in any question, is the importance and advantage and duty as well of knowing another man's position, and especially if that other's is your opponent's, as we say. I often think, in saying so, that we speak wrongly; because, although an opinion may stand over against ours and be contrasted, and, therefore, in mere locality or position be opposite, or opposed, it may not be what we offensively mean as opponent—inimical and destructive of ours. Your neighbours across the street are opposed to you, but they are not opponent. Now you may suppose that there is not any analogy; but there is a very deep and true analogy. I need not remind you that the phrases "opposite" and "opponent," and all others of that class, which we look upon as purely moral or intellectual, have arisen from physical position and locality—from this position of men and things to each other in space—in a street or otherwise. The people opposite meant, not precisely people who thought differently and did differently—in fact, who were in every way, intellectual and otherwise, set against you, just as their houses are set against yours. They were simply over against you in locality. But men, from being over against each other, or merely opposite in position, fall into the curious mental and moral state sometimes of changing this simple space relation into an intellectual one. You have your opposition benches in the Houses of Parliament —bitterly and apparently irreconcilably opposed in temperament and opinion—although there, space relations are as little different as can be, and although they have the advantage of changing places often. There was our old Scottish-border opposition—our modern Rhine opposition. Of course, in mere opposition in space, we look upon different things, or upon the same thing, differently. Your neighbour opposite has the sun in his rooms, and you sit in shadow; he sees the stream of people going down the street, and you see it going up; things that you cannot see at all —that your very position, as I said to you quite lately, would not allow you to see—he can see (perhaps by considerable straining we might get a glimpse of them, but who cares to make a strain and twist his neck to see what an opponent sees?). And then you see things that he is as little in a position to see. And you can understand now, without my going further into this and away from my subject, how, in all respects, the analogy holds between somebody across the street from you, and a man across the way from you in an opinion. The people whose houses we look into are our opponents, seeing what we cannot, and seeing what we can in a different way than we do. The people whose opinions we look across at are our opponents, but in the same sense—seeing what we cannot, and seeing, occasionally, the same thing in a way that we cannot. There is this great difference, however—that our neighbours over-the-way we treat quite neighbourly and frankly, and not as opponents, which they really are. We are not quite so frank with our intellectual neighbours over-the-way. In fact, my friends, we are on such good terms with our neighbours opposite, that we go across to their windows and invite them to ours, in order that we may each have a good honest view from the other's position. I hope we shall gradually learn to do the same thing in opinion—go in the friendliest way to our opponent's window, looking upon him as a neighbour over-the-way, and see things as he sees them; invite him cordially to ours, and show him what we have been long looking at. If we did this, we should settle a great many things, public and private, more wholesomely than we do—more thoroughly, and with less waste of feeling and energy of all kinds. That is by the way; but I found myself bound to tell you why I thought an opponent was not an opponent, but a good neighbour on the other side, seeing another quarter of the heavens than we do, and with a slightly altered view of things on the earth to what we have, and why it was the next best thing for us carefully to learn what he saw. It never is to your advantage to carelessly gather his views, nor to carefully misrepresent them; but you will find profit of the highest kind in being as scrupulous in stating his, as you are in stating your own. By so doing you may have to alter your own—adjust them slightly—and you do not like that? I believe there is much truth in this. We are all very much disposed to get, or take advantage of our opponent: the best advantage, however, is not to wound him in some unprotected part, but to let his strongest point tell powerfully on our weakest. That is a queer kind of advantage, but it is the kind we can most effectually receive from him. The other and common one is no advantage in the world to us, but a very serious disadvantage.

Now the mischief said to result from the impracticability of the religious and Christian ideal is put in this way: "In violent reaction against the utter selfishness of life . . . . it has insisted on a life utterly unselfish. . . . . But the misconduct of ordinary humanity, as now existing, is not to be remedied by upholding a standard of abnegation beyond human achievement. Rather the effect is to produce a despairing abandonment of all attempts at a higher life." The mischief goes much further, it is said; because it is added, that "by association with rules that cannot be obeyed, rules that can be obeyed lose their authority."[1] That, you will allow, is well and admirably put. The mischiefs of this ideal are twofold—despair of progress towards it and abandonment of the attempt, and a falling away from the point we have reached. That is, it produces a positive injury on common and current morality, and prevents the attainment of a higher—both very alarming and disastrous evils. It must be allowed that in our religion an ideal of life and society is held up to us which we do not anywhere see signs of being realized; that, whether in violent reaction or not against the utter selfishness of life, it insists on a life of unselfishness. There is one thing I cannot agree with, however, and it is not consistent with my experience, that the current teaching in our Christian pulpits and elsewhere has been anything like this ideal of Christianity. I do not imagine that any one who has much or long experience of what is commonly and widely taught in morals, can say that the Christian ideal as put just now, and as, beyond all question, put in our religious books, has been constantly and without variation insisted on. If there is the mischief stated, it comes from some source other than the common teaching of this standard. So far as my own knowledge goes, I cannot say that my recollection of teaching which I listened to for many years and from a great variety of men, and the account of religious teaching which now reaches me, is of the character described—that is, that it ceaselessly upholds a standard of abnegation beyond human achievement. I shall myself plead guilty to trying something very like this —to an endeavour to represent to you what I think is on the whole correctly described as the Christian, unselfish

[1] Spencer.

theory of life—an endeavour which I have felt for many years it is the one duty of an expounder of Christian teaching to make, if that teaching is to be known or felt. I am quite prepared to consider whether such a course, looking at the world as it is, is a wise course—whether it will have the results I have mentioned to you, in causing men to abandon the attempt of gaining the prize my text speaks of, and in causing others to abandon a life a long way off from this prize, but a life which is moving towards it. I think it is not possible to hold that the insisting on this ideal has had these serious effects already upon our individual and social and national life, and simply because, although we have had the ideal in our Bible and in Jesus, as a matter of fact it has not been insisted on, and, as a point within your own experience, as a rule none of us have been induced, by the pressing home of this unselfish ideal, to abandon in despair all attempts at a higher life. If in the past there has been much or little of this throwing up of the sponge, it has not been because the utterly unselfish and impracticable view of life has been so dinned into our ears, that in sheer weakness we have given up the struggle. But while this is quite erroneous as a matter of what is taking place around us—while there is no evidence that, because of the standard usually held up to us in moral teaching, we have given up all effort after anything higher, and in some cases sunk below what we had reached—let us see whether it may not be true that, should such a style of teaching become universal—should the pure ideal of Christianity be persistently forced upon men's attention, the result would not be as stated here—no improvement in morals, but rather a falling off. This is no new point, by any means, forced for the first time upon teachers of morals, although it has been put, and put very forcibly of late, in the way I have said; and although there is an under feeling in many of our minds, and sometimes a misgiving that there is great force in it. I shall put it to you as it was put to a great teacher some thousands of years ago, and give you that teacher's answer to it, because it will help to make clearer any remarks I may offer. "Lofty are your principles and admirable, but to learn them may well be likened to ascending the heavens—something which cannot be reached. Why not adapt your teachings to cause learners to consider them attainable, and so daily exert themselves?" "A great artificer," replied the teacher, "for the sake of a stupid workman, does not alter or do away with the marking line." This is the clear objection to an impracticable ideal—the feeling that it is asking us to scale the heavens, and the very impossibility of it taking all power from our limbs, so that we cannot climb the lowest height. And this is also in the main the answer to such an objection—that the thing to be aimed at is not to be altered or done away with because some may not hit it, nor even because all may fall short of it. I do not know how it is with great artificers and the bulk of workmen, but I imagine that in a great majority of cases things do not answer to the marking line; that although line and plummet are in use, many erections are not perfectly plumb. When we set a child to learn writing, we put before it a specimen which I am sure, if the child could use images, it would say might well be likened to ascending the heavens. As a matter of fact, we do not find that it abandons the effort in despair. It may never reach the impracticable ideal shape and shading of the letter. I don't suppose one of us here has; but it attempts the heavens, my friends, as you know, and attempts them with a lightness of heart and a persistency of purpose that, when we look at what is reached and what is striven after, make us astonished, and will sometimes make us smile. Its exertions are not daily, but hourly, and the feeling of fruitlessness is lost altogether, apparently, in the delight in the effort of attaining what we call the unattainable. You teach shooting, not by fixing a point which at the first or second or hundredth time every man will make. Few make points, and these few not often; but we never think of turning the entire surface of the target into a bull's-eye. But, you reply to me, and the reply is correct, that the young gunner has seen the heavens scaled; although he may be far from it, there are men about him who have hit the mark; and in this way the hopelessness of his first attempts is encouraged. The thing is seen not to be quite impracticable; by perseverance, he has assurance that he may reach it, as others have done. There is much in that; but that is not the sustaining power in striving after what is at present out of our reach. I think it is more in what our Bible-writer suggests. We are, if we are in earnest in the matter, not quite disheartened at the prospect; we are elated with immediate success; we mount on the top of this success to a point beyond, and every stage yields pleasure in the sense of ground won and an aim achieved—it may not be the ultimate aim. But, I suppose, it is an experience of young marksmen that the pleasure of first hitting the target, and the delight of scoring within the circle, will bear a fair comparison to their feelings when the spot is pierced. And in moral efforts and in religious culture, which, I have said again and again, and see every day more evidence of—which, we forget, is as much a branch of culture and education, and careful study and application of means, as any branch of training that belongs to human nature,—in this culture it is not out of place and not injurious, I think, to set up a standard or type beyond the actual, to hold before men an ideal after which they are to strive. What is to give spur to effort and pursuit in this, I think with all calmness, the crowning pursuit of men and women—what is to give spur to it, if not an aim beyond us, which we may not reach perhaps, but which each day will bring the feelings and actions of the whole of mankind nearer the type of perfected human life and character? It appears to me that there would be more to lead earnest men and women to abandon every effort after a higher life, were the standard fixed at what they could easily reach. In education, I find you can quickly produce carelessness and slovenliness of work by fixing the requirements sufficiently low. And in the Christian ideal, high as it is—in the clouds, to most of us—although, remember this, it has been made human—we have seen it in flesh and blood—like the young gunner I spoke of, we have here also seen the heavens scaled by Christ, who was "man and one of us,"—this high ideal is more likely to arouse the moral feelings of humanity, as it aroused those of the writer of these words, and give to men the fire and energy which belong to a fleet and healthy nature; so that, never once thinking to rest in what is attained—which, without a true ideal or any lively sense of it, I am persuaded so many do—they forget what is behind, and reach forth to the things which are before. It is true—and this is, I imagine, the truth in an objection such as I have stated to you, and in the feelings which we sometimes have ourselves—it is true that we must not discourage early efforts—that the man furthest from the height must not be made to faint at the sight of what lies before him—that he must be cheered and encouraged—that to cheer him and give him heart, intervening heights are to be first attacked and won; but to his inner eye, if out of sight, the summit for which he presses must be more or less steadily in view. That inner vision of the height beyond the height may bring dismay sometimes, but it brings also elasticity and hope, the sense of something to be achieved; and every upward striving, and, if it is steep and rugged, every inch climbed, proves that the achievement is possible. I am supposing ordinary moral health, not moral degradation and lassitude. "Let us not lead a common life; let us be active in a worthy manner." "It is incredible," says a man of my acquaintance, "what a cultivated man"—he means every way so—" can do for himself and others if he has the heart to act as curator for many, if he leads them to do at the right time what they would all like to do, and leads them to their ends, which they mostly have correctly in their eye, the ways to them alone failing them. Let us conclude a confederacy upon this—it is no hot enthusiasm, it is an idea which can be right well carried out, and which often, although not with clear consciences always, is carried out by good men." And that is, in other words, my friends, the Christian ideal.

V.

16TH NOVEMBER, 1879.
Evening Service.

HEB. ii. 10.—"For it became him, for whom are all things, and by whom are all things, in bringing many sons unto glory, to make the Captain of their salvation perfect through sufferings."

THERE is in this language, with which we are all so familiar, a very great principle set forth. We miss many great thoughts in our Bible, often incidentally expressed, and chiefly because the sound of the words and phrases are so well known to us, that they awaken no sense of their significance. There is a reason for this, and I could explain it, were I not afraid that it might prove wearisome. It has a perfectly natural explanation, and, to be very short, it is somewhat like this. Each word in the verse I have now read to you, and each clause, is a symbol of a great many things. When I read them, there is a vague, very vague sense of what may be symbolized, sufficiently intense, however, to make the whole intelligible, although not sufficient to take you into the writer's confidence, with whom every symbol awakened a lively image of something accompanied with strong emotion. There is excited in us no lively images of anything, and we are not aware of any accompanying feelings. We feel wearied sometimes. We may as well acknowledge it. We must have this sense of weariness. It is perfectly natural. It is the inevitable physical result of sounds falling upon our ears and producing a merely general sensation. Reading an interesting book, where the thoughts are vividly apprehended through the symbolic words, and when you follow the intensity of the writer and have his inner life repeated in yours, is sometimes so exciting that it will drive away sleep. The head is filled with images, the heart beats high with feeling: the words are no sounds in your ears, but magic spells that rouse the sense, and transfer to you the mental possessions of the man who uses them. In another state of mind and with another kind of book, few things will sooner set you to sleep than reading or being read to, although beneath the words there are, if we came at them, thoughts that leap and burn. Suppose you are from home, and your wife and family left behind, and you receive a short message from a friend—"Your house is on fire: wife and children and everything consumed." You have no dull sensation and inclination to sleep, unless perhaps the blow is so great, and the inner excitement so strong, that you are paralyzed; but this is from the very vividness of the impression. The words are not symbols. They are flame and blood. You are on the spot. You hear in them the crackling and hissing of the fire. "Your house on fire!" It is not a phrase. It is the crash of falling beams and the roar of the devouring demon. "Your wife and children consumed!" Good God! it is not language. There are in your ears the cries of voices that drive you to despair. Why! on the paper that you hold, it is not words you are looking at. There is your wife's face, resolute but pale. "And children!" You do not read—you see their frightened looks. One cries, "Father!"

You hear it most distinctly, and through the fire you clutch at it; and some one finds you with the message in your hand, pressed to your breast. That is what I call reading with proper fulness—not hearing the sound, but going straight to the sense, and having the very reality before you which the symbols set forth. Now you read another message. You are in very great comfort. It is Saturday, with a short and pleasant day's work. You have had your dinner, and the house is comfortable. You read a telegram also, not addressed to you, but addressed to an indiscriminate public through the newspaper, that in the South Seas twenty-three men were devoured by sharks. It barely raises an idea in your mind, and produces nothing that one could call a feeling. You pass on and forget all about it. Fiji is a spot on the map to you. It may only remind you of your school days. The natives you have a very dim notion of; but twenty-three, or twenty-three thousand, or less or more at that distance, and with that knowledge and sympathy, cannot move the imagination. A shark is an animal that you do not see in your waters, and the name has little more effect on you than a letter of the alphabet. And thus you can, without being called callous—because it would pain you to see a man bitten by a dog—you can fall asleep in the middle of the telegram. The extreme horror of this painful scene, the struggles and the agonies of the men, the ferocity of the monsters, the despair and desolation in the homes, are veiled from your eyes. You enjoy your tea very well and are very lively; but had you seen the spectacle which is behind these words, it would have been very different. That is more an illustration than an explanation of how we often read—the explanation being a very tedious thing; but, shortly stated, it is a want of imagination, and sometimes of sympathy, and sometimes of exact knowledge, or all combined. To feel with the writer of my text, to enter into his thoughts with his feelings, we must have more than a sense that there is nothing wrong with the grammar of the sentence—more than that the verse is put in an old-fashioned way; we must know more exactly and in detail than we do, what he means by a great many of his expressions. We attach no intelligible meaning to many of these expressions, or we assign them wrong and inadequate meanings—sometimes uncertain, traditional meanings. It is necessary for us to break up the language, which is somewhat artificial to us, and make some attempt to get at the real living sense. The words are far too general, too abstract, and we do not know what things are included under them. The phrase, "it became him," has, if we take it to pieces, a most interesting and curious and instructive history, and this man's words are not quite apprehended by us until we vividly know that history. The phrase, and the circle of thought under it, in these words, "through whom are all things, and by whom are all things," it is next to impossible for us, reading as we do, to anything like fully fill out to ourselves. We do not stop to know what he means by "sons," what he wishes to convey by "glory;" but he had very definite things in his mind when he wrote these words, and you must own that they are to us very vague and indefinite. And the idea of "Captain" was to him a great reality. To us it is a figure of speech only, with hardly any sense of reality. The notion of salvation, which our Bible is filled with, is by no means a clear conception in our minds. I should like to collect the meanings and the absence of meanings entertained about it. But salvation was a living concern to this man, and to the Captain of it a very clear and definite something. I am not exaggerating when I say that, to many, it is stripped of all, or nearly all, kind of reality, and become a term in theology without much relation to life. And so it comes about, as I said, that although the words are perfectly well known to us, there is all the difference between our feelings in reading them and this man's in writing, that there is between the father reading the telegram I spoke of, and our reading the paragraph about the South Sea islanders. We cannot put life into the words. They are looked upon as a theological opinion, and perhaps, therefore, very respectable and interesting to men who are theologians, but not to men as men. Now, if this were the case, I would leave the verse where it is, and not call your attention to it, because you are perfectly right in supposing that everybody cannot be interested in theological opinion, just as every one cannot be interested in other ologies. But it is a great mistake to suppose that this is a mere theological opinion—that the ideas in the verse are artificial. It is a momentous human opinion, and a great universal and natural truth. I should not trouble about it else—not in this place, at all events. We are concerned here with what is of general human interest—with what appeals to men as men; and this very theological-looking doctrine lies nearer the life of us all, than a great many other opinions that a nation will fall into convulsions over. Does it not touch on the great problem of suffering in human life, and offer some solution of it? Does it not more than suggest the question which I was speaking to you about last Sunday evening, and which is a burning question in religion and in morals, and one that we are in much need of rightly apprehending and knowing how we should practically stand to? It directly brings into view the Christian ideal, and its place and meaning in human life. If there is one thing that has made statements in the Bible, or out of it, void of real interest to us, it has been the absence of any attempt to show their connection with men's lives. We have come to this stage in our religion—and it is a great advance—that we desire from others, and are earnestly seeking for ourselves, a true reckoning of the opinions it contains. We are not satisfied about any matter being what is called religious; we must see the reasonableness of it as well—or, as I may say, the naturalness of it. If religion and its truths are to have any hold upon mankind, the time is fast approaching when they must make good their claim to this at the bar of nature and reason. They must be shown to be the true outcome of the human heart, produced by and answering to certain qualities in our nature and in life. We are only beginning to be aware of this, and dimly to understand what it signifies. The ideal, and Christ who is here spoken of as the embodiment of it, have had little or no effect upon our lives, because, although we felt, in the way I speak of, that we should have some reasonable account of this ideal and the character in which it was set forth, we have failed often in obtaining what we sought. We were told, in fact, that rational explanation was out of the question—that the peculiar excellency of the Christian ideal and of the work of Jesus, and the whole conception which you have so admirably summed up for you in my text, were, that they rose above rational explanation—that they were removed quite out of the sphere of what is natural, and belonged to the supernatural—that they contained something—and that this is the distinctive singularity of

Christianity and Christian thought—that they contained something superinduced on nature—that Christianity did not arise out of man's life, but that there is a foreign element introduced—an appliance for the advancement of the race which is not native to the race—that a great and superhuman effort, which we are not too closely to inquire into, and which is solitary and exceptional in the world's history, was made for the world's redemption. It is this, I need hardly say, artificial view of history and of a great religious and human idea, that is beginning to stagger some of us. We are daily finding it more difficult to throw ourselves heartily into this view of things. I think I may say, that we do not with any kind of heartiness appropriate this conception of the "greatest transaction in history." Nor need we, nor should we, do so. It is, however, high time that, with some sort of heartiness and intelligence, we threw ourselves into the reasonable and natural view, and recognized that the great, and what we may call superhuman, effort for the world's redemption, was essentially the working out of a principle of human life—that it is an appliance for the advancement of the race native to the race—that although, in the scale of it, it stands alone in history, in the spirit of it, it is far from being solitary and exceptional—that it is the result of the true working out of principles in our nature—that these principles are in operation now, and slowly making for the end, here mentioned, of bringing many sons into glory.

I shall not notice to-night the passing allusion in the verse to a great and profound moral truth—of men being perfected through sufferings, and especially of a Prince and Leader of the world's healing being prepared for his task in this way. It needs more consideration than I could give it, because a proper consideration of it would take us far beyond the commonplaces one hears and makes regarding the purifying power of suffering. The writer means a vast deal more than is implied in these. He means, and I can only hint at it to-night, that the formation of a life such as he here portrays—that is, the creation of all that we have recognized as finest and noblest in character—is in the nature of things—(that is what he understands by, "it became him")—by the constitution of man and the essence of goodness, effected through suffering. To fully show how this is, would be to exhibit to you the growth and development, under proper conditions, of a soul like Christ's—to introduce you into the schooling and disciplining undergone by this unparalleled Leader and Prince of men. And that wants time, my friends, extraordinary patience, very minute analysis of the inner life, and, in fact, claims more than one has perhaps any right to exact from you. I shall pass, therefore, from the process to the result—to the character of Jesus—to the unselfishness of life which he taught and showed—to these as the ideal, not of religion, but of humanity—to the captaincy of Christ as, what I called a little ago, a universal truth, and not a theological opinion—a fundamental moral principle. If this is the case, it removes one great offence which the captaincy of Jesus, as a bringer of salvation, has given to many, by taking away, what seemed to many, the unnaturalness and arbitrariness of the means; and it goes far to completely answer an objection like the one I stated to you last Sunday evening—that the continued insistance of the Christian ideal would paralyze moral effort, and men, instead of becoming better, would become worse—just as some people have declared that the extreme laws against drinking in the State of

Maine, instead of leading to sobriety, produced one of the worst forms of drunkenness, namely, excessive and hidden indulgence; although, so far as the last statement would go, I can safely say that all my observations in that State led me to the conclusion that the drunkenness must be very hidden indeed. I sought long and found very little. Nor do I think we should be more successful in finding cases where, from the high standard erected in Christianity and indicated in my text, men have fallen from a tolerable state of moral attainment to one below that. But I wish to make out more than this to-night. I wish to show you that what this writer says, and what is the rationalized statement of the whole act of salvation as we see it in Jesus, is the law really of moral growth; that its insistance does not merely not stand in the way of men and women becoming better, but that it is the great means of their betterness and of the improvement in the world which we see; and that the greater and greater acceptance of it is the condition of human advancement to the goal which it is making for—very slowly, as some of you may think, but still making for, and, with whatever speed, nearing somewhat. That is what the writer to the Hebrews calls glory. This old word, like a great many old words, has also little or no meaning for us morally. Religiously, when we hear word of being led to glory, we wonder, first of all, if the man is sincere, and what interesting human thought lies behind the expression, or if there is any. In your own language, my friends, it is simply perfection of character and life, to use the well-known phraseology of the day, which after another nineteen hundred years may be as hard to understand as this word glory. It is the development of the highest life in us, the true unfolding of all that is best in man. You know yet and use the pure Greek word doxology; that is, literally, "speaking glory"—we add in thought, "to God," and we use the word exclusively in that sense. We never think of a doxology to a great man or a good man. God is for us the Being in whom the highest is manifest, the One who gathers in Himself all that is most worthy of praise, all that is glorious, the All-perfect. This, then, is what men are to be led to, viz., to doxa—to a condition where you could sing them a doxology. I do not see why, since you use this word in combination with another so familiarly, I may not, without offence, quote the original. And I do this for the reason already stated, in order to show you how, under this old-fashioned and theological-looking text, there is a new-fashioned and purely human thought and aspiration. Glory also may have some fixed meaning in your mind when you dissociate it from much that is commonly connected with it, and realize it in its pure moral and religious significance, as that which sums up all that makes God to be God, and constrains all that is good in man to praise Him and give Him worship—that also towards which men are travelling, or being led, and which it is the work of Christ to lead them to—this Captain of well-being, Prince of a regenerated and healthy and sound humanity, this Guide to the complete and perfected life we worship far off in God—called, therefore, in the simple language of the human heart, and in no scholastic tongue, the world's Saviour, man's Deliverer, Chief in the effort to bring about the world's redemption, the Leader of humanity to ultimate perfection, to the doxa that we can only now ascribe to God himself. That, let me say in passing, in spite of much that you hear, is the only thing that is really glorious. There is no glory in leading men, even in the most brilliant manner, away from the perfection of life in God—none whatever in a captaincy that does not bring health and quickening to men and society.

Now the contention of this writer will, I trust, be plain to you. It is just the opposite of the able modern writer I spoke about last Sunday evening. That the Christian ideal, not only held up as a far-away aim for us, but embraced and worked out by us, is the way to bring men to what humanity is striving for—to what, I said, all men of every persuasion earnestly desire to see it reach—glory, as this New Testament writer understood it— fully formed virtue, completely developed life—the highest goodness and godlikeness, as we prefer to express it; that, without this utterly unselfish theory, and the serious practice of it, any little movement towards what all consider a higher and purer moral life could not have been made; that, in fact, it is, so far from being simply ideal and impracticable, really the only practicable and working conception of morality possible for us. It is not meant for a state which we have no conception of. We usually postpone it under this belief. We say, society is not ripe for it. In saying so, we only repeat objections which we hear, without duly weighing them. You are to hold this manner of life before the world, neither looking for it in yourselves nor others in the meanwhile, and because it is too early a-foot! Is help, my friends, too early a-foot to support a man who is falling? Is it too forward to think of rescuing a man that is drowning? You would see him safely on shore before you put out your saving powers? You would have the sick man whole before you gave him advice and tried your healing skill? Really we have been talking words without a particle of sense. Christian unselfishness and abnegation, love for others, healing of society, deliverance from its mischief, leading it on to perfection, are to be, in the mean time, put aside, and we are to come out with all these feelings and powers, and put them forth when everybody is unselfish and ready to deny themselves—when there is no malady in society to cure—when it has no actual evil from which it needs deliverance—when perfection is reached, glory attained, and no leader necessary! You will lead men when leading is not required, leaving them, meanwhile, in a difficult road and with heavy work, captainless! Why do we not postpone the study and practice of medicine until men and women have reached a normal state of health, and are not liable to disease? Why does not the brave general hide himself until the battle is past, and come forth and display his virtues and shout "glory" when the last blow is struck, and, with weary eye and tremulous hand, the brave fighting men respond? The writer from whom I have taken my text has an entirely different notion. My own notion is very different. I am so far from thinking that Christianity is an ideal and impracticable thing, that I believe it to be a purely working scheme of morality—not the most impracticable, but the only practicable morality—the condition of the advancement we have reached, and the sole condition of all future progress. It is essentially the scheme for the state of things in which we at present live, although we have not been in the habit of considering it in this light. It is most realistic—and now, and only now, in the absolute form we have it, to be practised. Not to be delayed until a perfected society comes into existence. In a perfected society and in "glory," as we say, there may not be room for it. Saviours can only do their work where the people need to be rescued—not when the rescue has been made, or after men have saved themselves, and there are none to be delivered. Physicians, this great Physician himself said, are only for the sick. When men are healed, and women and children, and the perfect state has come, the physician's occupation will be gone. When the sons of men have come to glory, the Captain's commission will expire. Unselfishness and abnegation, if they continue after this, will be very unlike what they are now.

Another and entirely different view emerges here, and one which may surprise you at first hearing of it, but which will bring some comfort to those who dread the Christian notion because there seems no end to the denial of oneself, to the sacrificing your own for others' good, to the parting with what you have, that others may have more. It is perhaps simply, my dear friends, not an endless thing but, as I said, a working and temporary and realistic plan which must pass away, as the conditions die out that give occasion for the exercise of it. We have named it wrongly. It is not ideal, impracticable, but only real and practicable. The healing art must end when disease has ceased—leadership drop when the task is accomplished. There can be no Saviour when all are ready to be saviours: there would have been no crucifixion had all been Christs.

VI.

23RD NOVEMBER, 1879.
Morning Service.

JUDE 3.—"The common salvation."

I REMARKED last Sunday evening that we did not, for reasons which I then gave to you, quite understand our Bible—that, although we might always perceive that the sentence was intelligible and correct in form, we failed often to penetrate to the thoughts of the writers—that their feelings in writing, and ours in reading, were hardly commensurable.[1] We are all, I suppose, aware of this. There is an intensity and earnestness in the writings which we do not catch in the reading. The men were clearly interested in the matter with which our Bible is occupied, in a degree in which we are not. I gave you an instance of this in the great doctrine of the Christian Church; and I had occasion to say that the idea of salvation, with which the Old and New Testaments are so full, did not by any means occupy the place in our thoughts that it occupied in the thoughts of the men who wrote these books. And the cause of this mainly is, that we have wrong ideas, or no idea at all, as to what salvation is. It is looked upon by many as belonging to a peculiar and separate experience, marked off and set aside as the religious—as something that may enter

[1] Sermon V.

into their life, but as something that may not, and life be, on the whole, very much the same, whether it does or not. It is sometimes, I fear, regarded as an idea to be realized by emotionally religious people only; and the chances are, if we heard a man at a street-corner speaking about salvation, and another at the opposite corner speaking about the growth and treatment of potatoes, we should not hesitate a moment which of them we should listen to. If we were challenged, we should say in perfect sincerity: The question of potatoes is a plain human question, and one of great importance to the whole population; but if there is anything human in this other matter that is on some people's lips, we cannot see it, and at any rate it is not so urgent as the potato question: it can rest a little. I think, my friends, when you have thought more round the question of salvation, you will find it human enough, and to include not only the potato question, but all questions whatever relative to the true welfare of mankind. We do not see this just now as we should see it, and men may cry themselves hoarse at street-corners and elsewhere until we see it. Perhaps the men that cry out about it would need some enlightenment? No doubt they would be the better for it. I believe many of them also have a very vague notion of what they are offering to their fellow-men. It is one of the most precious and largest gifts that humanity can receive; but they conceive of it, as we mostly all do, too artificially and unnaturally, and whatever is so regarded cannot appeal to the human heart. Men are right, although they are not always quite sure that they are in the right, in preferring potatoes even to that. It is no use for any length of time to say, "Why, sirs, it is a matter of religion, and religion is all-important to us. You know the words of Watts—about its being the chief concern of mortals here below?" That will not do. Which of you believe that it is so? and which of you, believing it—for you are all honest men, and act up to your convictions—which of you, believing this, make it your chief concern? I say it is no longer advisable to hold this language: "Salvation is a question in religion, and religion is a very momentous affair. You should, as reasonable men, weighing affairs of greater moment with those of less, give earnest heed to the matter." If that is all that can be urged, I have no doubt that potatoes would still have the preference. We feel the importance of potatoes; we do not feel the momentousness of the common salvation. We do not know quite certainly that it is momentous. We have instances in the Psalms and in some of the Prophets of the enthusiasm and passion it could kindle—of the songs it could inspire. You have example sometimes of the music it has given birth to. But what feeling does it awaken in us like that which it awakened in Isaiah? We can read the words, and sing them, and in a sense enjoy them; but how much reality have they for us? and how far sincere should we be did we ourselves write, "How beautiful . . . . are the feet of him . . . . that publisheth salvation"? I think, to be perfectly honest, we are moved more by the publication of many other things than we are by the announcement of this. And I do not see why we should not be honest and say it. It does us all a great deal of harm to hoodwink ourselves, and to keep up feelings that are not perfectly natural to us. Let us confess to ourselves that we would rather listen to something about potatoes than to words about salvation—that we feel the one comes home to us, while the other does not—and we may then come to a better understanding with ourselves. We shall then ask, and expect an answer, why it is that this is the case. And we shall go further, and ask, if salvation does not come home to us, nor concern us so much as potatoes, why we should be so solemnly asked to attend to it—why men of old were so inspired with the idea of it—why institutions exist for the publication of it? All questions, my friends, greatly needing to be answered. For if the matter is so important as our Bible men say it is, and show so plainly that with them it actually was so—if it is so important as the machinery in churches, ministers, missionaries, lead one to consider it to be, it is not consistent with these things to display so much real apathy as is done. And there really is, as every one who thinks the matter over will acknowledge, a great deal that is not very consistent in all this. Either the apparatus is out of proportion elaborate and extensive for this idea, or the feelings of by far the vast majority of men and women in Christendom in regard to this conception, are infinitely below what they should be. On the one hand we do so much, and on the other we do so little. There, judging by chapels and churches, one would think that salvation was all that the old prophets and Jesus said it was—here, judging by men and women, one has to conclude what we have already seen to be the actual position of the subject. I am not astonished at the perplexed attitude which these things show us to be in, in regard to this question, and, in fact, in regard to the whole question of religion. It is an attitude resulting from two things—the lingering notion in our minds of the importance and sanctity of religion and of all truths connected with it, and the growing feeling that many of them have not any vital union with man, or, at least, that this union is not experienced by man. In deference to the first notion, we keep the machinery going that has always been in existence; and in obedience to the personal feeling, we cannot exhibit the devotion to the purposes of religion which a Jesus and a Paul manifested. Salvation is not to us what it was to the Hebrew poets and prophets and the New Testament men. It fails to arouse our interest and engage our affections—to give inspiration to our thoughts and energy to our actions—and simply because we do not understand it as they understood it. It had for them, personal human—social—world meanings that it has not for us. It inflamed their thoughts not less than the telegram I mentioned to you last Sunday evening would do in the circumstances I imagined. They read behind the mere word, things that we do not read at present. Salvation is a word to many of us and nothing more—an opinion which it is the duty of men like me to speak about and call people's attention to; and there is a dull sense of duty in listening to it. But we are not able to see its bearings on life—we do not discern, with anything like clearness, what it has to do with society—what there is in it to make any one say with human heartiness and absolute sincerity and naturalness, "Salvation, oh the joyful sound!" There is many a piece of intelligence that we hear, and of which we can frankly and honestly speak in this way; but how often is it in our own heart to speak thus about the common salvation, and how often do we actually say this, not because it is really in our mind to say it, and our hearts are full, but because it has been written for us and set to music? Now, I know you will not misunderstand me so far as to think that I mean you are not to sing and to read any statement but what you yourselves would give expression to. I have no such meaning, because singing and reading in my opinion, are fitted to excite or deepen the sentiment. I know this, I say, and I shall not guard myself from such a misunderstanding. I only wished to let you see, in a way that you can all understand, how it is with us in this matter, viz. that we do not enter into the thoughts and feelings of men who wrote about salvation so as to be able, naturally and heartily, to respond to them. And this is, as I hold, not from want of sympathy with the men, but from a misunderstanding as to what they meant, from an erroneous conception of what salvation is. I am quite certain that if the men and women of our day knew what salvation was to prophets in Judæa, and to the great Prophet of Nazareth above all, their hearts would heave at the thought of it, and their throats scarcely give passage to the volume of feeling. Once they can be made to forget the narrow and inadequate idea which many of them have as to what the word stands for, and realize the broad and perfectly human conception which it had originally, and which must again be claimed for it—nay, we must claim a broader and more human basis than even that—once they can do this, we shall not only sing what prophets wrote, with the feelings of prophets—we shall write songs of our own about it, and, unlikely as it may seem, we shall have music of our own. For songs and music, like the birth of everything else, have their causes in the nature of things. The conditions existing, Nature will send her bard to express what every heart is full of, and her music-master to give relief in sound to the pent-up feelings of her children.

And what is, you ask, the human idea in this salvation that we imagined to be a Church question? You will have to go back with me a little to see this. You are aware that it occurs in the Old Testament as well as in the New—some of the writers there talking about it more enthusiastically even than those in the New. Now, between that time and ours there lies a great space, but not greater, I believe, than the difference, if you will permit me to use space measure, between their idea of salvation and our own. I said I should like to gather the meanings we entertained on this subject, and the no-meanings. Am I wrong in saying that in many cases the word is so abstract and stript of meaning, so away from fact and living reality, in our minds, that it is more a collection of letters whose pronunciation is familiar to us, than the symbol of what most dearly and intimately concerns us? At the earlier time I speak of, it was not more abstract, or hardly more abstract, than the word potato. That, you know, is more than a combination of letters. It brings something into your minds that is very real. Well, my friends, salvation did so with the early Jews. You would hardly credit the amount of valuable information to be got by tracing the history of a word. You will obtain a view of changing manners, government, modes of thought and belief. It is sometimes like the epitome of centuries. I do not profess to say that you will find all this in the word we are speaking about; but it has a history too, and a few observations which might in a dictionary look very uninteresting, will, with the object we have in view, not be, I trust, altogether so. I have often occasion to notice to my Bible class how moral and religious and spiritual words began first in uses quite different from their present. They meant material and physical things. And salvation, which we have removed somehow out of reach of all that is material, and very much, as we have seen, out of reach of what is earthly and human, is as good an example as any. So much had it originally to do with man—and although we have altered its meaning somewhat, I hope to convince you that it has still to do with man, and in ways most akin to the nature of man—so much has it to do with us, that it signifies at first to be spacious, ample, broad, and is, you can see, of noble, even if physical, parentage; and it has not, as we shall see by and by, brought discredit on its origin. It has retained through all its changes, as its distinguishing and qualifying feature, the sense of amplitude. Now there was in the Hebrew mind, as we can gather from a great deal of their language, a very close connection between mere physical spaciousness and opulence, and moral liberty or freedom from danger and distress. Breadth and amplitude, even in space, gave them, as it must do all free people, the sense of soul liberty and security. Illimitable forests and prairies would be the highest good to the Indians. They would understand the root conception of blessedness being placed in this. And then the opposite idea is quite close at hand, that confinement and narrowness of space are equivalent to distress and danger. We still speak of straitened circumstances, of ends not meeting, and we know there is little amplitude or blessedness in the life we so describe. This breezy word was used by and by to describe many states besides the merely physical one of width or even comfort. It came to mean, quite naturally, to give width, amplitude, I doubt not, in the physical sense first, and then in a higher sense to set free. And, as you know, a certain amount of space is necessary to the maintenance of life, it came to mean to preserve—first, again, I dare say, to preserve the actual physical life of men in all dangers, and then to preserve something better and finer than the physical life. You can observe how gradually we are leaving the ground and ascending to higher and remoter meanings. It is used also to signify aid and succour in general, and at first, and when correctly used, either physical or moral aid. I shall read you one or two passages from the Psalms to show you how natural and human, and with both meanings, the word is employed. For, my friends, we must not forget this, that the moral life is to be attended to no less than the physical, and the physical no less than the moral—that religion does not consist in neglecting either—that salvation, which is the last word in religion, includes both. "He shall save the children of the poor." I am very much tempted to enlarge on some of the Hebrew modes of salvation, but it would take us too much away from what we have before us to-day to do this. You will suffer me, however, to point out to you that here you have one direction that the common salvation will have to take—and this is not, you are well aware, a thing foreign to us and to society, but a matter, as I can testify with grief, pressing sorely upon society. And it is very likely that when we try to bring in the common salvation, we shall have to fall back upon the parentage of the word, as I termed it, and first of all realize the primitive physical meaning, and let the poor children realize it, by giving them space and breadth and amplitude of life. "Save me for thy mercies' sake;" "Salvation belongeth unto the Lord;"—where the meaning is more a moral one, but including the other as well, and in both cases signifying something natural and human and social. "My king cometh unto thee," says one of the Jewish prophets; "he is just and having salvation .... lowly." What I wish you to observe is that, here and elsewhere, salvation is as much connected and concerned with the common life as justice and lowliness. This "having salvation" is rather,

I should imagine, being saved himself, enjoying the amplitude of life I spoke of, and therefore able, and he only being able, to give it to others, as his justice is the guarantee that he will deal as a king should, and his lowliness that he will bear himself as few kings have done. The word goes on to give expression to other shades of meaning, and we have from it directly deliverance, aid, safety, welfare; just as we make from, to deliver, our word deliverance; from to save, safety. "Let the God of my salvation," or help or deliverance, "be exalted." You have then the names of actual deliverers, such as Joshua—and the name of the great Christian deliverer, Jesus—both directly from the word, and retaining the original meaning of it. Joshua, a national deliverer, saving his countrymen from the dangers of war, and leading them to a settled political and agricultural life, in which what was good in the people had free scope for development. Jesus, also a deliverer, national, it is true, if his nation would have followed his lead, but really a world-deliverer. The historian who mentions his name, gives also, as you may remember, the reason for so naming him, and the reason is what I have told you—"Thou shalt call his name Jesus, for he shall save his people from their sins." He emphasizes, you observe, the moral deliverance, thinking it, with perfect justice, the most important, and including every other form of deliverance. But that is not what I wish precisely to note in the carrying over of this actual name and thing from Jewish to Christian times. It is the human aspect and entirely natural conception of this salvation which I wish you to note; it is its actual bearing on life and society; it is the fact, which I am afraid we continually miss in religion, that we are concerned with a great social reformation—that salvation means your deliverance and mine from every evil, and our introduction into a fuller and ampler life, physically and morally, æsthetically and intellectually—deliverance from whatever is straitened, and therefore hinders the growth of the individual life in goodness and well-being, including every form of it that we are capable of—beginning in the lowest, in which the word took its rise, and proceeding to the culture and the preservation of what is best and noblest in us. And this not for ourselves, my friends; but this for the world—this, especially, for the many wretched specimens of humanity which are everywhere to be met with—toward this, as they have capacity to go forward, and as we have the heart and the will to guide them.

Jesus interpreted his name and his mission and the common salvation in a wider sense than his biographer Matthew. He included Matthew's sense, as you know, and made many an effort to lift his contemporaries out of their sinfulness—not to save them from the consequences of their sins, which is an artificial notion we sometimes entertain—but endeavouring a far nobler and more moral act, to save them from the power of sin. He came to call sinners to repentance, to inspire them with his own love of what was good, and pure, and lovely and godlike. But he came in the full powers of a true, world-wide and human deliverer—with all the amplitude and spaciousness of nature and of aim that lie in the conception of his purpose of salvation—to raise the fallen, heal the sick, give sight to the blind, to inaugurate a movement in social life which is essentially the improvement and elevation of men and women in the widest and fullest sense that the most intelligent social reformer and lover of his race can conceive. It means that hundreds and thousands of our population should not live where they are now allowed to live, and should not live as they live—that ignorance should cease—that vice should end—that industry and its fruits should be regulated; it means, that you and I should be like the King, just and having salvation and lowly, and should then with might and main try to save others. Shortly, it is this—and here is the intense humanity of this common salvation and the reality of religion—that nothing foreign to man is foreign to it.

VII.

30TH NOVEMBER, 1879.
Morning Service.

ISAIAH xi. 2.—"The spirit of knowledge and of the fear of the Lord."

I NEED not conceal from you, my friends, that I have been for some time back aiming more directly at what I have all along, more or less indirectly, made my aim in teaching here, to engage you on the side of religion and religious effort. And I have done this lately, or endeavoured to do it, by what I may call the argument on the reasonableness and naturalness of religion, and particularly of Christianity. I refer you to my morning discourse of last Sunday as an instance of what I mean;[1] but I might as well refer you to all my morning and evening discourses since my return from my holiday in the beginning of October. I have no wish to give this out for a novelty; for there is one thing you may make sure of, that almost everything you may say, thinking it the newest and the best that has been said on the matter, you will find by and by, if your reading is extensive enough, has been said much better than you can do, and years, probably centuries, before you. The world of thought does not begin with us; but there is this curious thing about past expressions of true thoughts and fine emotion, that you may not perceive

[1] Sermon VI.

them even if you meet them, and may not find pleasure in them when you perceive them, until you have first learnt to utter them for yourself. That appears to be the curious condition of human labour in this field. You trust to get to some true conception of things, and put your conception in words, and when you have done it, you are astonished to find how much better it has been done before you; and you would now very gladly make use of another man's words instead of your own. I could, for example, find you instances as early as the ninth, tenth, eleventh and twelfth centuries of Christianity, not to speak of much earlier times, where the thoughts which are usually called modern, and pass as "advanced," were much clearer and fuller expressed, and evidently more thoroughly weighed, than they are now. I make no claim to novelty, therefore, when I call your attention to the form in which I put this argument on the reasonableness of religion, and when I desire you to observe that it is not exactly like the way in which it has been put to us in later days. When in the seventeenth century men in England talked—and they talked a great deal then—of the naturalness of religion, and of Christianity founded on reason, and so on, they occupied different ground from me. Some general truths in religion, such as the existence of God, for example, and the common and obvious moral duties of life, were, in a way, demonstrated without, what the men would have called, the aid of revelation, but built up solely, as they gave out, by an elaborate process of thought. I need not tell you that this has not been my way of setting about showing you the naturalness of religion and the entire reasonableness of the great truths in Christianity. I have accepted what we call our revelation. For this, every one must see, is a fact in the history of religion. I have accepted this just as I receive other records of human experience in the past, and my desire has been to make clear to you, that the phase of life brought out so prominently in these books, and which we call spiritual or religious, is a true and natural side of human life and thought—quite as natural as the moral and physical and mental—that what many were beginning to have hesitation in maintaining, is a wholly unquestionable element in man's life and history, and that the expansion of this part of his nature has proceeded, and is still going on, in accordance with laws and under conditions that are open to men of discernment. I have been especially desirous to show this, so far as regards the moral aspect of religion and the great virtues of Christianity. For if there is one thing, after our natural repugnance to the line of life which Christianity sets before the world, that has been found more objectionable than another, it is the opinion, not grounded, nor attempted to be grounded, that the model it draws of what men and society should be, was not based on a due consideration of the nature of man and the exigencies of social life; that the thing was, in short, the outcome of imagination and enthusiasm, begotten by men of this temperament, and now and then expressed by the same class of minds, but a thing that could not lay hold of the world, because it had no footing in what we term the constitution of things. It did not rise naturally out of the existing condition of affairs, but was sought, in a high-handed manner, and under great and, what certainly had become for most men, solemn sanctions, to be imposed upon it. Now, as I said to you the other Sunday night, that view of anything will not pass muster with thoughtful men. What astonishes me sometimes, however, is to find that many thoughtful men suppose this to be the sole view of the question, and think that they have disposed of the whole subject by disposing of this view. You have disposed of a false and most injurious aspect of religion in doing so, but the true and rational and natural side of it remains. What if men have understood Christ wrongly, or at least inadequately—have misapprehended the true universality of salvation and redemption[1]—have failed to grasp the full significance of his moral standpoint as a human and a natural one! What if they have talked, in a way that was losing much of its meaning for you, about revelation and inspiration, and about God! What of all that, and more than that? Is their misapprehension, or inadequate knowledge, to draw you away from a truer and more perfect acquaintance with these things? Because the light is feeble, you will wholly put it out! You will judge of this matter by what the weakest has to say for it, and not by what it has to say for itself, or by the strongest. It is this on the moral, or what some of you would call the practical, side of religion, that I have been endeavouring to bring before you. And on that side of it, I am bold to say, no man can escape the obligations of it by saying that the scheme is not feasible—that it is not consistent with nature and human life. It is the only feasible scheme before the world at present, as I hinted to you one Sunday evening lately,[2] and there is not another carried out by us, or proposed to be carried out, which is anything like consonant with life and nature, and at all answerable to the circumstances in which society at present finds itself. And I may go further and say, that in the inmost and most truthful

[1] I need hardly say that I do not mean here what is called Universalism.
[2] Sermon V.

corner of our hearts there is not a man or woman who has thought over the matter but will fully bear me out in what I am saying. But enough for to-day on this aspect; and more, really, than I intended. Religion has a side that is concerned with knowledge as well as life. Not but that the matters I have been naming must be known as well as lived, and lived the better the better they are known. But the facts in connection with religion and the religious life, are matters for observation, and comparison, and thought, and form, or may form, a body of scientific knowledge, exactly as we have a science of other facts connected with man, or with the physical world. This of course is a natural consequence of the view which I have been telling you of. As soon as we discern that religion is a natural and inevitable expression of the human spirit, and has a history and a growth like that of thought in general, or morals, or industry, or society, we discover that, like these, we may have our science of religion, explaining, so far as our observation extends, the nature of it, and the laws that have governed it, and the conditions under which it exists at present, and under which it will continue to exist and advance. Hitherto we have had a body of knowledge in connection with religion, and which went by the name of science. We have had, and have still, our theological science. I don't think it has been in great repute for some time. It has been made a butt of by almost everybody—by capable and incapable people alike. And it is not difficult to do this. It is a much more difficult thing, when you come to ask what is the matter, and how you are to remedy it, to make reply. It is seen that it is wrong, but it has not always been seen where it is wrong, and why. It has been wrong, to a large extent at least, in not emphasizing what I have been speaking about—in not observing the entire naturalness of religious life and thought—in not, therefore, leaving room in its system for all stages and degrees of that life and thought. It accepted what I may call the high-handed theory of religion, and proceeded to elaborate its doctrines in what some have felt to be an arbitrary and plainly dogmatic manner. It could not help itself. The system was suitable to the prevailing thought of the time and the common discernment of the subject, and could not be otherwise than it is. We could not wish it otherwise. It also is a true history of the human mind, and we are where we are with the help of it, and, some of you suppose, with its hindrance. Well, I shall as little question that; but hindrances, or what we call hindrances, are sometimes real helps. You all know the uses of a heavy drag coming down-hill with impetuous horses. Good drivers and prudent passengers know the value of it.

Now I need hardly say that this is not the form of knowledge which I wish you to identify with religion. I would not have you to despise this, as it has become the fashion to do—not at least until you have conscientiously studied the matter for yourself, acquainted yourself with the history of this kind of thought and the men who shaped it. I may say with certainty, that when you have done this, you will not be in the least inclined to speak contemptuously of it—you will find more in it than you were led to suppose. Not exactly what the men believed to be in it; but something less than that, and something also considerably more than you yourself have been led to believe is in it. The knowledge we are to think of in connection with religion is a branch of the great tree of human knowledge. This is something that we have not all felt it to be. It has been, as I was saying about religion itself last Sunday morning, looked upon as outside of everything distinctly felt to be human. That, I imagine, has been the feeling in regard to it entertained by a great many among us. We felt, as in the case of salvation, that we ought, from the high authority of the subject, to pay some heed to it; but we were at a loss to give a plain reason why we should do so. Agriculture, the science of agriculture, we know and feel is indispensable. The matter interests and engages men, and we see the reason for it at once; just as, on the practical side, we saw immediately that the produce of agriculture in the shape of potatoes had, beyond question, a claim to our attention which we were not certain that salvation had. Mechanics and engineering are known to be branches of knowledge of great human import, and are pursued with the full sense that they are so. These are felt, even by men who know nothing of them, to have a near connection with what is human. Geology, botany, chemistry, astronomy, and the more practical kinds of knowledge rising out of these, in mining, medicine, navigation, are immediately seen to be useful and human sciences. The science of trade called political economy is acknowledged to be intimately allied to what concerns man and society. There are others which I need not name to you—jurisprudence, government—and we are sensible, although we may not know one of them, or only one, that they are, one and all, natural branches of knowledge, as we say, and spring directly out of man's relation to the world or to his fellow-men. We at once accede to them a place among the subjects which we may and must pursue, as human intelligences seeking to understand the matters we daily have to do with in the affairs of life. There is the crust of the earth we walk on, variously composed and curiously arranged—we desire to know the meaning of it, and how it came to be as it is. There are flowers and plants scattered all over the crust; we are pressed by some inward impulse, not only to arrange these and name them, but to understand their growth and formation. There is a somewhat involved social and trade life in which human beings are engaged; we must not only engage in the traffic, but as reasonable men we must have an explanation of how this came about—how it maintains itself, and how it can be best maintained and furthered—which, as you know, is in other words to say, we must have an ordered knowledge of what lies before us in a disordered array of facts, and that is simply a science of the facts. We have not felt the same thing in regard to religion. There are not many, whose duty it is to deal with this subject, willing even to hear of such a thing. The name, Science of Religion, is unpleasant to them. I can very well remember a highly cultivated theologian, whom I once had occasion to consult on some matters of this kind, being very much hurt at the expression. He seemed to think it would give rise to misunderstanding, and would be to many an extremely offensive phrase. And the cause of this is not far to seek. If we have not quite come to see that religion, in the practical aspect which I have been for some time speaking about, is essentially a matter of human experience—every bit as much the outcome of the true nature of man, even as trade and government and laws have arisen from his social and other instincts—if we have failed to see this, we must fail to understand how religion can be a science. The two go together. If you keep to what I call the highhanded and arbitrary view of everything religious—if you do not see that salvation, and the other matters with which it has to do, are most completely human—no man will make you see that you may have, and must have, a science of religion. And, as I said a little ago, the actual condition of the question is, that hardly any one believes that the thing is possible. And there is then the further fact, that hardly anybody has, what may be called, a human interest in the science of religion, or sincerely thinks that it can be humanly interesting; exactly as I showed you we had lost the hearty and quite natural interest in the practical matters of religion, which we read about in the Old and New Testaments, by our regarding the subject as in no way appealing to our hearts, and a long way removed from our natures, and the concerns which, as men and women, occupy our thoughts and our active intervention. I shall say, for myself, that every day I see more clearly that no other matter is so human, in the best meaning of the word, and no other branch of knowledge is so intimately connected with man. There is not any use whatever in teachers of religion and religious people complaining of this want of interest. Men will not be interested merely because they are told they should be interested. I could not, at least. When I came to the evening service last Sunday, I passed a man in a lane, whom I hear usually about that hour; he was then screaming, with what seemed excruciating earnestness, something about what "the Son of God had done before all eternity." The man must have had some human thought in his own mind before he could have worked himself into the state which he evidently was in; but my own feeling, as I hurried on, was, "I want something nearer to me than anything that the Son of God may have been said to have done before all eternity;" and, "God help these poor people if that is all that is offered them to draw them to the gospel and the religion of Christ!" Let men see that it is veritably of interest to mankind—make them feel that, without question, not as a matter of authoritative statement, but as a matter of fact and of their own experience, religion is all, and more than all, that has been said about it, both for them and for society. Let them see—I do not suppose it can be done all at once—but let them gradually learn to look upon it and the many facts connected with it in its long history in every quarter of the world—in India and China, in Africa and America, in Greece and Rome, and ancient Germany and Scandinavia, no less than in Judæa and in modern Europe—as genuine and natural expressions of the human spirit, with reference to a world and an order of things which lie behind what we touch and taste and smell and see. Realities! if ever there were realities in the universe. Human! if there be such a thing as humanity. Humanity, in the delicate essence of it, is not, as you well know, in rocks or atoms or flowers, in machinery or agriculture, in trade or government, nor in the knowledge of these—not in what appeals to any of your senses, but in what appeals to your spirit. And reality, after all, is not in these things either, which look so real. I shall not say, as some have done, running from one extreme to another, that there is nothing in these things; but there are times, and these our best times—there are moments, and these the most critical and the most solemn in life—when there is a movement within us that makes us brush aside these things as impertinences in what is truly manlike, and compels us to reach to the reality that we see behind them, and with which alone and with the full intensity of life the spirit can close and find rest. First, I say then, let us feel that the facts are facts of human life, and particularly of human life, where the humanity is most clearly uppermost. Interest in a practical way will follow, and the pursuit of the knowledge and source of this phase of human life will no longer be regarded as it is—as worked out, and only to be worked out, apart from human experience, and to be excluded from the domain of intelligence, because outside the sphere of intelligent action. It is but beginning, and can hardly be said in our country to have taken a beginning. It was, therefore, with no small regret that I read the flippant and contemptuous remarks of a statesman who has earned the title of being called great, but remarks which show all the more how dangerous it is for any man to pass beyond his boundary of knowledge, and hazard an opinion on what he knows nothing about. It is not my custom, as you know, to take notice here of matters that are spoken about elsewhere; but there are cases where the rule must give way. And where a man in a high position, and commanding the ear, and in some cases swaying the opinion, of many of his countrymen, gives expression to sentiments that are perfectly wrong, it is a mere matter of duty to put the thing right. I have no doubt that there are many people who will accept Mr. Bright's implied conclusion about religion and the future of it, including the teachers of it, which he was good enough to bring before a body of school teachers in Birmingham a little ago. That conclusion was plainly this: that there was very little in what ministers of religion had to teach to the people; that their influence, by their own confession, was as good as nothing; and that the future of the country was in the hands of the schoolmasters. Religion, as a branch of knowledge, was, according to him, as good as what is vulgarly called "played out," and the separate inculcation of its practical precepts by duly qualified men a thing of the past, and to give way to the carrying out in the country of the fourth standard. Spoken by an obscure man and a completely ignorant man, no one would ever read the speech; but nothing more ignorant could hardly well be spoken about a subject. Teachers of religion do not accomplish all they might accomplish; but that is owing quite as much to the common opinion entertained about religion, both as a rule of life and as a subject of knowledge, as it is to the men themselves. The statesmen of Holland are much more intelligently informed on this matter than many of ours, and have quite recently asserted, in a practical way, for religion what I am now claiming for it—a place among the great human sciences, and a place at the head of these, by establishing in the highest schools of learning chairs for the teaching of the history of the development of this phase of human life, and for the discovery of the laws of its growth—teaching in which, as in all human sciences, the results shall not be tested by churches and by show of hands, but by reason and truth. This, you will see, hardly fits in with some movements on foot among us; but there is in this a truer vision into the future of religion and of humanity than we in this country can lay claim to at present.

VIII.

30TH NOVEMBER, 1879.
Evening Service.

1 CORINTHIANS iv. 5.—"Therefore judge nothing before the time, until the Lord come, who both will bring to light the hidden things of darkness, and will make manifest the counsels of the heart."

THERE can be very little doubt, I think, that the early Christians—Christ's own immediate followers in particular—thoroughly believed that he would come again, and probably in their lifetime, and take the position which they saw rightly belonged to him, as King and Ruler, and especially as Judge. There are a great many passages, both in the Gospels and the Epistles, which clearly show this, and it is not quite fair to attach another meaning to them. To do this gives us no help to understand our Bible and early Christian thought. For if there is one thing that requires to be brought home to our minds just now, in connection with an intelligent understanding of the Old and New Testaments, it is that the writings in both are strictly historical. What I mean by that is, that they arose quite naturally out of the state of mind and opinion and whole condition of the times to which they belong—that there is nothing in them which we may not understand and account for, provided we know exactly what I have called the state of mind and opinion and the condition of the times. You will get to the meanings of the different writers—their phraseology, their distinctive ways of putting things—as you get at these matters in other writers of the past, by searching into the antecedents of the men, and by forming a true picture of the life and thought by which they were surrounded. New Testament literature and thought—and it is, we shall have to acknowledge, a somewhat extended literature, covering a great many various authors, as you know, but also covering a great many years—New Testament literature and thought are to be explained in the way we would explain the literature and thought of the middle ages, for example; or the literature and thought of the last century, or of this or any century. It is through a true estimation, proceeding on a precise knowledge of all the facts of the time—social, religious, political, commercial, mental, moral. We have not looked at our Bible in this way. We have looked at it very much as a thing standing, as we say, on its own feet—an isolated thing, having nothing to do with any matter beyond its two boards—solitary, mysterious, unaccountable. Solitary, in a sense, it is—even as great goodness is solitary. Mysterious, too, in a sense—in the fact, viz., that what I have called its naturalness, includes a view of the nature of man, which we are very slow to allow; but neither solitary nor mysterious in the sense that it is unaccountable.

And this notion of the second coming of Christ was one of the ideas that mark for us the period at which these books were composed, fix their position, recal their historical character as the product of what I may call the combined forces then operating in that part of the world through these writers' minds. At another period, and in another country, the idea could have had no place. It was an idea made up of several parts. First and foremost, it had its root in the then peculiar notions entertained about the soul, and its mode of existence after death, and its occasional return to the theatre of its previous experiences. It borrowed something also from the great Jewish conception of a Messiah, as a ruling and all-powerful monarch. I say great, because it is one of the grandest poetical and religious conceptions ever cherished by a people. It was quickened, too, by many remarks made by Jesus, and inadequately understood by his followers. For we must have noticed that his aim, in the pure spirituality and extent of it, was not known nor sympathized in by the men he had attracted to him. And the idea was besides intensified and made vivid by the disappointing conclusion of Christ's life, and what seemed the complete collapse of his followers' expectations in him as the promised Messiah, who was to lord it over all their enemies and utterly subdue every opposing power. The hopes he had awakened of national and religious revival, and the sudden extinction of these hopes, or apparent extinction of them, by his own overthrow, added to the influences I have already mentioned, and working in the minds of earnest and imaginative men, would soon give rise to the idea I am speaking about. Many felt the force and goodness of the personality of Christ. They saw that what was best in the Messianic hopes of their greatest writers was united in the young Galilean. Could such power and goodness come to nothing in this way? Must the hopes of the select spirits in their country and their own hopes lie buried there? Has that heroic effort—the most heroic they had heard of, or that we have known—has it spent itself in death? They could not believe it. His purpose could not be so frustrated. Peter sounds the note of this new expectation: "The God of our fathers raised up Jesus, whom ye slew and hanged on a tree." God's work could not end in that way. The event for which the ages had been preparing could not be strangled at its very bringing forth through the ignorance and passion of men. This we all feel. Things must march on, let men do what they will. And so Peter says boldly, and in the thought and language of his day, but embodying, as we shall see, a true and universal belief: "Him hath God exalted with his right hand to be a Prince and a Saviour." "Know assuredly," he said to his audience, "that God hath made that same Jesus, whom ye have crucified, both Lord and Christ." The thought went on repeating itself in various writers, and became sharpened and more clearly defined. "And as," one says, "it is appointed unto men once to die, but after death the judgment, so Christ was once offered to bear the sins of many, and unto them that look for him shall he appear the second time without sin unto salvation." And gradually there gathers round the idea imagery suitable to it, and borrowed from the great solemnities on earth, and with which later Christianity is more familiar. "For the Lord himself shall descend from heaven with a shout, with the voice of the archangel and with the trump of God, and the dead in Christ shall rise first." "And to you who are troubled, rest with us, when the Lord Jesus shall be revealed from heaven with his mighty angels, in flaming fire, taking vengeance on them that know not God, and that obey not the gospel of the Lord Jesus Christ." Men's hopes are in no way dashed, you see, by the calamity that overtook the Child of Hope. They take a new and as yet unheard-of swing. The Messianic hope has been spiritualized, and the personality has been exalted, in a way that early prophecy knew nothing of. "When the Son of Man shall come in his glory and all the holy angels with him, then shall he sit upon the throne of his glory, and before him shall be gathered all nations;" and then you have all the imagery which immediately suggests itself on the mention of such a scene—the separation of the nations in the way a shepherd would divide his flocks. For this great Judge is a great shepherd too. Or, as you have it elsewhere, And the books were opened. For this great shepherd is a supreme Judge.

Driven by the natural course of things from a literal and physical interpretation of what their great thinkers had handed down to them, and what Jesus seemed to realize, his followers seized upon a wider and truer conception of the work and mission of Christ. They are, in all I have quoted to you, very plainly a great way off still from what I called the spirituality of his aim; but they are nearer it than when he taught among them; for the possibility still was there that he meant to ascend the throne and become a veritable ruler on the earth. Even in that highly coloured physical imagery about the second coming, and the evident thought behind some of it of a personal rule on the earth, there is unmistakably a moral conception of Christ's work and mission—faint, I acknowledge, but the beginning of what has been making itself clear in Christian thought, far, as yet, from being thoroughly clarified. Essentially we retain the same imagery. The grandest expression of this idea, and in some respects the grandest outcome of the Christian conscience, is built up entirely upon this early and New Testament view—I mean the piece that is commonly called the Dies Iræ, the Day of Judgment. It is the true continuation of the glorified moral conception of Jesus which I have noticed as springing up in early Christianity, when the first idea was forced to yield to the pressure of events. But if you read it—and you will find a good translation of it in our Hymn-Book, number 1051—if you read it, you must see how the thought has been deepened, and what it has gained in moral meaning, and in insight into the true purpose of Jesus, and in discernment of his character. I do not say that it gives us the final reading of these things—far from it. It has not been able altogether, although we can see there is a noble Christian struggle to do so—it has not been able entirely to steer clear of the mere drapery of New Testament thought. It has allowed the simple imagery to colour the essential conception, and in the fifteenth and sixteenth verses we receive something like a shock, and, in fact, they run counter in a great measure to the spirit of the piece itself. But, on the whole, we have nothing like it in, what I may call, the moral poetry of Christianity—nothing that so well expresses one of the deepest thoughts of the religious mind, and the great underlying conception of all the Titans in literature and art. I hope some day the Christian spirit will do something better; but in the mean time it is simply without parallel. Had we been quite in sympathy with this great work of religious genius—and I hope in course of time we shall have sympathy with every expression of thought in the past which is honest and sincere, however unlike on the outside it may be to our own—had I been sure of this in the present case, I should have taken the liberty of asking our excellent conductor to let you hear the piece in music. For you yourselves are well aware how the choir can speak to you through music, in tones of contrition, of awe and of ecstacy, and thus awaken religious feeling and emotion in a way that the human voice in speech, or the mind in pure thought, can lay no claim to.

But now I dare say you will ask, Why all this about the second coming and the Dies Iræ? Simply, my friends, that you are in that part of the ecclesiastical year called Advent, and this is the first Sunday of it. The Christian Church still keeps alive the thought of the early Christian people. We do not profess to keep this ecclesiastical year; we observe, at least, only some events in it. I don't know how much the worse we are for it, or whether we are any the worse; but there is one thing I would beg of you to note in regard to it, that I do not think we are any the better for not doing it. I have no intention at present of introducing such an observance. I prefer, in the mean time, to make use of it when it can be made useful, and when it cannot, to let the occasion pass without remark. But there is great use, I consider, in the observance of this season, not simply in order to perpetuate the ideas I have been describing to you. Some of you think, very probably, that you cannot join in such a thing. You suppose that the thought which is commemorated has become obsolete—that very few people, if any, really entertain it. It is one of those religious conceptions which you have begun to look upon as purely arbitrary, quite artificial—perpetuating what I called in the morning a mere high-handed theory of the universe, or part of such a theory. It appears to you one of those matters in religion which look so unnatural and foreign to what belongs to men and women, that are bringing religion into disrepute and great neglect. There are many things which you are willing to call to mind and to keep in remembrance. Religious ideas of this kind, however, that rest on fancy and mistake, and not on truth and nature, are best forgotten, you think. But, although peculiar in its shape and in its images, it sets forth, my friends, a great and solemn truth in religion, and therefore in nature. I have spoken so much about this of late, that I will not go back upon it, and I think I may be at liberty to say now that whatever is religious is natural; and if we once recognize this, we shall be able to go the further step and see that whatever is natural is religious as well. This, then, I repeat, is no artificial and mere theological idea. It is a moral, religious and natural conception, one discerned by all ethical observers, and the groundwork of the greatest efforts of the human mind. It is the realization of this thought in the tangled maze of human events, and the more or less clear exhibition of it, which made the Greek drama, and which has given our Shakespeare his pre-eminence in the universe of thought. The idea that behind all there is a judgment, unobserved sometimes, sometimes denied, slow, uncertain, or swift and sure, but in the end and somewhere to be faced—inevitable, discriminating; as Paul admirably puts it, and as no one, not a Shakespeare, could more truly put it, "bringing to light the hidden things of darkness and making manifest the counsels of the heart." This is in plain words what the New Testament men and religious natures mean by judgment. It has been sometimes strangely put, no doubt—put in ways that we could hardly see the truth and naturalness of it, and mixed, in the putting, with much that was neither true nor natural. Its fundamental idea, however, all thoughtful men can see, and can pardon the shortcomings in the manner of expressing it. Who can express it? Who will venture to formulate it fully? We see sides of it only. Here, it seems clear that life is weighed and measure of judgment awarded; there, that judgment is postponed. Here, that it is overdone, and good and bad overwhelmed in one blind fate; there, that it is underdone. Judgment is delayed, we think, beyond all reasonable limits to this one; it is hurried on unfairly to that one. The hidden things keep in the darkness, and only now and then are the counsels of the heart laid open. "All friends shall taste the wages of their virtue, and all foes the cup of their deservings," says Shakespeare, feeling that it must be so, but barely making us feel that it is so, since Cordelia is dead as well as Regan and Goneril—since Lear is mad and dies, as well as Edmund, and Gloucester's heart bursts, and the poor fool is hanged; and, in short, as in Hamlet, the end is dismal—"quarry cries on havoc." Judgment hardly seems to sit in state, but rather "proud death to have a feast toward in his eternal cell." You are made, nevertheless, to feel this, in the seeming confusion of outward award of good and ill, that you would infinitely be good and affectionate and true with Edgar, and shiver with him in his rags and misery, than leap into the proud position of an Edmund, and face the outraged conscience. And Edmund himself feels it. Before he dies, he must worship goodness. "Some good I mean to do before I die." Who would not choose to be with Cordelia in exile, rather than with Regan and Goneril at the head of the government? She is drawn somehow, it looks, into the general judgment—basely strangled in prison; but there is a judgment within a judgment. And the inner judgment which is brought to light is this, that Cordelia had preserved the jewel of her womanliness; Goneril and Regan had "foredone themselves." The perplexity of outward events, and the promiscuousness of the common fate on the outside, turn us sometimes away from the truth that I speak of, and which the Christian Church has steadily kept in view, and the discernment of which, through whatever confusion, is the mark of greatness in a man. It is this that makes Job so far beyond his friends; and although he may fail sometimes in argument, we can see throughout that he has the right of the matter; and the book gives, if not the clearest—for, as I said before, absolute correctness and exact measurement are not to be spoken of in this connection—but if it does not give the clearest idea possible of a great human and religious fact, it gives one of the profoundest readings of that fact anywhere to be met with. The Christian Church has put it into a dogma, you know, and defined it to such a degree, and striven after so much exactness in the determination of the question, that it has, we feel, falsified it to a considerable extent. Judgment there is, but when, and where, and how, who shall determine? Must we think it settled here, and in one particular form, and visible? Must we suppose it quite delayed, and to take place yonder, also in particular form, and precisely on lines and according to familiar and resembling transactions among ourselves? I shall not take refuge in the inscrutability of the Divine judgment. I shall but remind you of the width and depth, and possible extent every way, of any true and wise judgment. I shall recal to you the experience of a man who, in one quite peculiar shape, which we do not always think of, felt this universal act of judgment:

> "When we in our viciousness grow hard,
> (O misery on't!) the wise gods seal our eyes
> In our own filth; drop our clear judgments; make us
> Adore our errors; laugh at us while we strut
> To our confusion."

But I do not wish to speak of the forms of judgment. They are innumerable. Nor of the grounds of them. They are not calculable. I speak to the fact: for it is to the fact solely that my author speaks. It is to the fact mainly, if not solely, that all authors have spoken, authors both in the New and Old Testaments, and out of them; and, I believe, in the Christian doctrine as well, although it sometimes looks far otherwise, it has been the fact, and not the modes of the fact, which has been in the minds of all the greatest. And here religion is at one with human experience, and especially with moral experience, as it is, when adequately understood, always and everywhere at one with it, but going deeper than common moral experience. And this is the true teaching of religion and human life, that whatever else is plainly manifest in the world's events, judgment is not concealed. There is retribution—not vengeance; but there is to virtue her wages, and to vice "her cup of deservings." The last penny will be paid to virtue; do not doubt that, my friends. Some people entertain strange doubts about it, and give strange reasons for their doubts. They have made up their minds, for example, that virtue must be rewarded with other wages than her own—with money, with success, with friends, with every comfort. That is, let me say it, extremely vulgar. You never learned that in any book of good culture or of great wisdom. Your Bible never taught you that; and although we do not know it as we should, and do not use it as we should, it has, speaking with perfect exactness, more wisdom than any book I know or expect to know. Shakespeare never gave you this illiterate notion of the wages of virtue. Virtue has her last penny paid to her, but it is in coin of her own, in money valuable alone to the virtuous, and discernible alone by them.

Virtue is the reward of the virtuous. The good has his goodness recompensed with good; and vice her cup, to the last drop of which she must drink. The great historical and actual idea, which is also the great moral and religious conception, of vice punished and virtue rewarded, is grander and nobler than the vulgar and popular story notions. And the final reward is no more than this: virtue to the virtuous—the highest good to goodness—the sight of it and the joy in it: "Come, ye blessed of my Father, inherit the kingdom prepared for you." We would rather have another kingdom. This is too intangible. I know that, my friends. It is what I have just now said. Virtue can only be paid in her own coin—in money which the virtuous only can estimate, and which they alone can discern. I have made these remarks on the strictly moral and retributive conception of religion, and of life and history, because I can see, creeping into the religion of our day, under a one-sided conception of Christianity as the religion of love, a view of life and of morals which is destitute of stamina, and without foundation in the great lessons of history and religion and common experience.

IX.

7th December, 1879.
Morning Service.

Isaiah xi. 2.—"The spirit of knowledge, and of the fear of the Lord."

I DID not say last Sunday morning all I had intended to say on the subject I then spoke to you about.[1] It is in my opinion a matter of very great importance—next in importance to the religious life itself, and a necessary condition of all healthy and intelligent religious life. It has not in any way helped religion to win the affections and control the actions of men, that the practice of it has often gone along with great ignorance in regard to its nature and its history. In all rightly-balanced characters, the fear or reverence of God must be accompanied with a spirit of insight, or discernment of the disposition in man on which this reverence is based, and a knowledge of some other things which I shall mention to you by and by. Of course, you will always meet with people who say, Give us the practical result, don't bother us with the knowledge that lies behind. For I find—and I dare say some of you will find too—that the desire for accurate knowledge of principles, in any given sphere of knowledge, is not a very strong nor a very wide-spread desire. But if you continue the passage that was my text last Sunday, and which I

[1] Sermon VII.

have again chosen, you will observe, that what looks like abstract and scientific knowledge, turns out in the end to be purely practical. The religious life is touched by it. "It shall make him of quick understanding in the fear of the Lord, and he shall not judge after the sight of his eyes, neither reprove after the hearing of his ears." A very practical consequence! Unacquaintance with the knowledge I spoke to you about will not make a man more religious. I have all along said something very different, as you know, and up to this point have mentioned little or nothing in regard to the Science of Religion. I have kept before you what, according to my text-book, is the religious life. But there is such a thing as an unintelligent and ill-informed religious man or woman: a man and woman, therefore, who, while having an understanding in the fear of the Lord, have not what the prophet calls a quick understanding—have not, in reality, what you will find given in the margin of some of your Bibles, "a fine scent" in religious matters—are without any presaging instinct and capacity of the sort that makes the horse descry the distant battle—capacity of the sort that, in its higher exercises, enables the prophet to anticipate the future, and in the present, in spite of what his contemporaries may say or think, to work and teach for that future. The great men and writers in the Old Testament are men with this quickened religious instinct. The great men in the New, and our greatest, are men who, in power to live and instruct religiously, were able, by I know not how long, to presage what is still future to ourselves. There has been, and there is at present, a great deal of dull understanding in the fear of the Lord—a great want of power of scent, religiously speaking—an absence of anticipation of the future in act and teaching—

of a future such as Christ and Isaiah have discerned and foretold, and which Christ at least forelived (if you will allow me to use the word). For, although we have an expression for a man seeing and saying what is yet a long way off, we have no word for a much more significant thing, for his seeing and doing what is still in the distance. But there is prophetic life as well as prophetic utterance—a doing beforehand as well as saying.

There are certain other drawbacks to a want of wisdom in the matters which belong to the religious life, but this that I have just named is by far the most serious—the blunting of the perception of what is spiritual—losing the keenness of scent in a great circle of human life;—a loss which has retarded progress in religion practically, and has brought many long ago to a complete stand-still as to any theoretical knowledge about it—in fact, as I showed you last Sunday, making even intelligent people call this kind of knowledge in question. But every one may see how any keenness of scent there might have been, has, for great multitudes among us, had the edge of it quite taken off; and taken off, as I maintain, and shall prove to you from time to time, in a large degree, because of the want of knowledge and intelligent information about the facts and principles of religion—facts and principles which ministers and churches should teach, but which our churches inadequately—I dare say very inadequately—hold up to the community. What institution, my friends, what branch of activity, what man of us, adequately holds up what we all nevertheless stand for? We men stand for sons of God—images of the divine. How inadequately we image the divine, I need not tell you. The State stands for, not what it is unhappily in actual fact, but for something greater and more beneficial than it is likely to become for many a long year. Trade and industry stand for something that our present condition of things will not help you much to frame a picture of. They are not there, as you might suppose from what you see, in order that each should make sure of obtaining as much of the good things for himself as he can. That is, of course, pretty much how matters are at present—very like what political economy would teach you they should be; but that is not the idea of them, nor anything like what they are to be, but quite the opposite of what they are to be, and will be—never fear it, my friends. They are to be institutions, not for each to obtain the biggest share of the good things for himself, but great and noble institutions, to enable each to distribute the greatest good to others. And churches also stand for something that will be. That they represent this inadequately, I confess, just as I confess with grief and regret that each man of us, the institution called government and the organization called trade, and others that will occur to you, fall infinitely below the idea at the ground of each of them. What is there—name to me one institution—which holds forth purely the ideal towards which they are all striving? The most sacred and the noblest, and perhaps the best maintained among us I shall mention—but who will venture to say that marriage, the union of a man or woman, is in existing wedlock realized in the purity and grandeur of the ideal which it faintly bodies forth—wedding of spirit to spirit—souls flying together—each drawn by the other's loveliness—unity of intellect and heart, and every spiritual good, for the purpose of maintaining and furthering each other's well-being in more than a merely physical way, and of leaving behind them better intellects and better hearts, and more capacious souls? But that is, my dear friends, something like the idea underlying home life. It is towards this—and I say again, never fear it—it is towards this that the squalidest and—let me not name it—but vilest homes are struggling. Precisely as it is in the direction of the rule of a King of righteousness, and power, and pity, and salvation, that the most brutal governments and the most thoughtless are going—towards the time when, as I have before said to you, the large and powerful nations, like great and strong natures, abounding in goodness, shall fit out ships and anything else that is necessary, and equip them in order to carry help to the weak, knowledge to the ignorant. I shall not enlarge on these matters to-day, because even at this time of day they almost appear to have as much of a prophetic character as they had centuries before the birth of Christ. What we want now is, what I said a little ago of Jesus, a number of men and women who will not only foretel the future, but, like him, forelive it—be doers of the future as well as seers of it. Now some of you may imagine that in the remarks about the science and teaching of religion, I wish to magnify my office and make much of my calling, having some fear behind, which is common enough, that its days may be numbered. I have no such wish and no such fear. The functions which I imperfectly fulfil do not need to be magnified by me or any other man; and as to the days of churches, and probably of religion being numbered, their best days are but beginning—hardly yet, to my thinking, begun. I do not say this of religion as it is now often understood and taught, and even practised. I do not say this of churches as they now exist; nor shall I venture to say under what form they have this better future before them. I am bound very little to any form;

the best form, to my mind, being that which is the most effectual instrument in communicating religious impulses, and imparting sound and accurate religious knowledge to the people. This may be in some of the existing churches, endowed or disendowed, Independent, Presbyterian, Episcopalian; or it may be in no existing church organization. If you take the matter of religious instruction in a nation —and I may say that I know hardly any kind of instruction that is so much required in our country, and for which, as I hope to show you on a day not very distant, so little is intelligently provided—if you take this question outside altogether the other questions which have been unfortunately mixed up with it, and look at it with some knowledge of the subject-matter, its nature and range—you will come to see that the settlement of it is by no means so simple an affair as some would make you believe. But, whether in any existing church or in one not yet existing, I have so little fear of the work not being done, that there is nothing of which I feel more certain in regard to the future. I do not mean the immediate future. In the immediate future it may be quite otherwise than what I say. But I feel sure that, through some institution suited to the thing to be done, the great principles of piety and religion, the deepest and tenderest sentiments of the human race, its greatest and truest thoughts, its highest and noblest aspirations, will be nourished and enforced, taught and illustrated, in a way that we have no idea of at present, and do not trouble ourselves to form one. So much about my office and my fear of its continuance. I hope you are all as proud about yours, and I am certain you need be, and may be justly so. I trust also that you can look with some degree of confidence on the unavoidable changes in the form and the spirit of your offices which the future has in store for them, and that you have some heart in working for this future.

And now, once more, for the subject of a knowledge in religion—a subject which I should probably ask you to excuse me for troubling you with. I know I labour under great disadvantages in dealing with a matter of this kind from this place. It is away, as some of you will say, and say with apparent truth, from your ordinary line of thought and sympathy. There are many questions, political and social, which we can be interested in; but this is one that we find very little interest in. We think, perhaps, it had better, like higher questions in astronomy, in biology, physiology, be left to properly trained and qualified men. If that were really your opinion, and the opinion of the great body of Christian and non-Christian people in our country, I should have nothing to say against it. I should perhaps agree with you, and not trouble you on the subject, or communicate ascertained results, furnishing you with authorities and illustrations, much as a man would teach you geology or philosophy. But you know that this is not the view commonly entertained about religion. You know that most people rather resent—and very foolishly and inconsistently, as you will see—resent the idea of any man, or body of men, being authorities in religious science. It is called an affectation of Romanism and infallibility. But it is just as much so as it is rank Romanism to place Kepler, Newton, Kant, Lyell, Murchison, in the position they occupy in their respective sciences. For as we recognize authority in the other sciences, so shall we, in time, be obliged to own authority in the science of Religion. And there are authorities, whether we recognize them or not. And I could name to you—only the names would do you no good, for there is not one of our countrymen among them—I could name to you men who are really authoritative on this science, so far as it has attained a scientific position. But, as we still look at the subject, a man who gives a little of his leisure to the facts and problems which it embraces, considers himself quite as good an authority as another who may have given up a great many years of his life to it. I may say quite frankly and modestly that I am not at all of his opinion. As things are, therefore, that is, while religious truths are supposed to be matters for everybody to have their say upon, and matters, apparently, opinions on which are to be weighed not by any sort of quality in the opinion, but mainly by counting heads, it is necessary that subjects of this kind should, from time to time, be dealt with in this place. I do not choose the subject. It is thrust upon me by the feeling in the public mind in regard to it. And when I ask you to bear with me in speaking about what is not of interest to many of you, I trust you will keep in mind what I have just said—that it is really put upon me.

I shall now give you some indication of what a science of the human experience, called Religion, amounts to. I shall take care not to enter too much into detail, and, in truth, the time at our disposal will not admit of this. And when you hear what I have to say, there are two things that you will be in no doubt about. The first is, that a little casual knowledge from a few popular works will never make a man an authority in this branch of knowledge; and the second is, that the time is not very near when our public schools and schoolmasters, as has been suggested, will supply this kind of teaching. And, to begin with, my friends, I must look upon you, and you must regard yourselves, as something like a body of scholars.

First of all in this field of knowledge, there is the history of religions—I mean, of religion everywhere—the account of its rise and growth and decay, if it has decayed—its absorption into other religions, or its modification by these. This will have to be done, not for the great continents of the world only, but for the islands and the remotest peoples. To do this, you can see for yourselves, implies a knowledge and an acquaintance with details which is probably not exceeded in the case of any other science. You must lay under contribution the hundreds of thousands of volumes on travel and discovery issued by all civilized nations; and you must carefully weigh the statements of travellers and judge of their credibility. It is necessary, in order to do this part of the work with any kind or degree of accuracy, to have a knowledge of the sacred books of the various peoples whose religious life and thought have to be set forth, where they have preserved any memorial of these in writings. It is necessary to know something of their monuments, to understand their symbolism; to know a good deal of their past history, politically and socially. And these are all points most difficult to become correctly acquainted with, and just most difficult at the place where they are most interesting and useful for the purposes of science. Past history is not easy to come at, even where we have tolerably full written records to go back upon. But with most of the peoples I am speaking of, there are no such records. Tradition is a guide sometimes; the spoken language may give valuable hints; the bodily features of the people may help us; their living and dying customs may occasionally point us the way; their manner of building boats or making huts, of burying their dead, of treating their young and aged, may all aid us. At present, this part, and most necessary part, of the science of religion is defective, and will be for a long time, if it ever is otherwise, on account of the great extent of the subject, and the difficulty, in many instances, in obtaining information, and the no less difficulty in getting a proper interpretation of information that may have been supplied. I can give you some indication of what is meant under a head of this kind, and so help you to form an estimate of the sort of work that lies before those who will undertake to be versed in scientific religion. There are two religions of which we have very full documentary and fairly reliable historical information, the Jewish and the Christian. The kind of inquiry I speak of, confined to Judaism, and not to mention any pre-historic study, involves a history, from the earliest date we know, of the Israelitish religion, and this must be based on a properly ascertained account of its wide and varied literature, the dates and occasions of the composition of each of its books, so far as carefully trained critical and historical knowledge can fix these. In the mean time, you are aware—and I wonder how many people actually realize the gross absurdity of it—you are aware that the work of properly qualified critics and historians is attempted to be come at by show of hands in what, as far as regards questions of this nature, is only a mixed mob—I mean church constitutive assemblies. You might just as reasonably gather a crowd from behind the Overgate and Scouringburn, and ask it to decide by show of hands upon the scientific value of the Copernican and Ptolemaic systems in astronomy. But further, in addition to these two points in the religion of Palestine—I mean the general history of it, and the account of its literature implied in that—there is involved exposition and explanation of the Old Testament thought. And to do this correctly and fully, it is necessary to have not merely a sufficient knowledge of Hebrew and other languages called Semitic; it is very necessary to have a grasp of the thought and religion and customs of these distant peoples and their neighbours in very remote times. What I have said has to be done for Judaism, has to be done for Christianity, its early history, the literature that sprung up and has grouped itself round that history—the exposition of the thought contained in it, involving, as everybody knows, a knowledge of Greek, but of a special form of it—acquaintance with systems of thought and belief lying far outside Palestine—in fact, a mastery of the culture and religion of the whole of that time—a branch of inquiry for which comparatively little has been done. And to complete the history of Christianity, it will be absolutely necessary to follow the course of its thought, which means carefully to study the writings that are called Christian, from the first century to the nineteenth. For you will discover that, to know the history of Christianity and its thought, you cannot stop with the Apostles, nor even with the Fathers, as they are called, no more than you can rest satisfied with a knowledge of the five Books of Moses in inquiring into the history of religion among the Jews. The work, you will acknowledge, is really a very serious undertaking, but it is more serious than I have given you any hint of. You are barely on the threshold of the preliminary study. What I have supposed done for Judaism and Christianity must be done for China. I shall leave you to guess what that means. For only a small portion of their important literature has been translated and placed in the hands of students of religious science, a portion that furnishes hints of the religious life of this most interesting people, but nothing more. And our subject is not concerned with hints, but with accurately ascertained facts. India has to be worked—a quarry in itself. We have here also instalments, but nothing approaching the state of knowledge, nor the means to that, which we have in regard to Judæa and Christendom. Africa has furnished us with many valuable facts; and from Zulu-land we had, some years ago, from a careful observer, very interesting and important information with regard to the religion of these people—in some phases of it, most touching and beautiful, and, I shall venture to say, bearing in mind what I have said before about religion, most true as well. Ancient Greece and Rome have materials to give us, but they require ordering, and enlightened interpreters. Ancient Germany and the more northern inhabitants in ancient Europe, as far as Greenland, have contributed a little. Russia and the related nations on the south-east of Europe have to be interrogated in the painstaking way I have indicated to you. Mahommedanism has to be studied as impartially as Judaism and Christianity and pre-Christian Germany. The great American continent, North and South, in which much has been done, has more to give us about its various and scattered tribes. Peru and Mexico, with their elaborate religions and high civilizations, have more light to throw upon our subject by the history of it in these parts of the world.

That is a kind of sketch of what I have called the history of this great subject in the different peoples and religions of the world—a mere sketch. And this sketch is, when filled up in its details, simply, as I shall probably show you on a future occasion, the introductory chapter to a subject bound up intimately with man and his history from the earliest times, when he felt the wonder and the mystery of birth and life, and looked into the darkness of death.

X.

7TH DECEMBER, 1879.
Evening Service.

ROMANS xiii. 10.—"Love worketh no ill to his neighbour; therefore love is the fulfilling of the law."

YOU have probably been perplexed about what we call strong statements in the New Testament, such as "He that offends in one point is guilty of all;" "He that loveth father or mother more than me is not worthy of me;" and the demand made of the young man that I spoke about two Sunday evenings ago, and the words addressed to him who had kept all the commandments—"One thing thou lackest." Mere extremes! we are apt to think, and, if I mistake not, we say as much. Or they are rhetorical arguments, to be allowed to earnest, and especially religious speakers. But, my friends, no argument is permissible that is not correct. And a rhetorical argument, if it is true rhetoric and worth anything, must be based on undeniable truth; otherwise it is worth nothing, and is absolute waste of breath. I should be ashamed of myself if, under the disguise or pretence of rhetoric or earnestness in religion, I said anything that would not stand in a pure logical syllogism. It will not do to get away from the expressions I allude to in this way. For, as I said once before to you, they are not accidental—they are quite deliberate, and, in fact, in harmony with the most essential thought of the New Testament. And that thought, as you are aware, is something like what is expressed in my text. Viewed in the light of this sentiment, the apparently strong statements and rhetorical arguments are seen to keep most strictly to truth and fact. There is not one of them that will not fall into place if brought under what I may call the category of Christian thought. What are sometimes called the excessive demands on men and women, will be found to be neither more nor less than a reiteration in various forms of what is known as the Christian principle of living—a principle which, as I said in speaking about the case of the young man, we are ready as a principle to approve of—which the world is very forward, as a principle, to acknowledge. Europe runs and bows the knee to Christ, and says, like the young man, " Good Master." I don't think there is any want of recognition of this description; the difficulty creeps in when a demand is made to give the principle shape and bodily presence among us; when in this man's case and that woman's we ask for a true application of it; when in our own personal case we feel the application insisted on. We can very probably go over the Decalogue with a tolerably clear conscience. And I am far, very far, from saying that it is nothing for a man and woman to be able to do this—that it would be nothing for our town and country to be able to do this. That would be a very great victory on the side of morality and order and well-being. It would be nearly all that a great many people are contending for, all that they think it worth their while to contend for, and probably in their opinion as much as can be looked for. And, in truth, when one sees the great need even for this, one feels the less wonder that so many should rest satisfied in the attainment of it. Compared with our present condition, the realization of this would apparently go a long way to the establishment of something like the Christian kingdom, we suppose. If we could only ensure a faithful adherence to the old Jewish moral code, might we not be very well content? For masses of modern people to pass muster in this very ancient standard, which we have heard sometimes was done away in Christ, would be a considerable movement in the right direction in the nineteenth century of the Christian era! This is, when carefully considered, a very remarkable confession; but it is, in substance, the confession—I do not know with what degree of sorrow, or if with any degree of it—of a great many earnest social reformers. The remarkable thing about it is that, after so many centuries of progress in the line of Christian thought and feeling, we should come to this—that we should resort to something long antecedent to Christianity, and consider it a blessing for our towns and for ourselves if they and we could be brought up to that level. On the other hand, it may be said, such a state of matters in our times, and such a standard of living in the early history of Judaism, say a great deal more than is usually granted for the insight and elevation of the Jewish mind. And so it does. But how does it bear on people who profess Christianity, and are familiar with the insight and elevation of mind of a Jesus? What is its significance for us who have taken this man as our Master, who nineteen hundred years ago said to an exemplary Jew, who had done all that we should like to see done, and would be happy if we saw it done—"One thing thou lackest"? Its significance is something like this, that we are losing sight to a great extent of distinctive Christian sentiment and thought. I have often made this a charge against our times, and here and there I have substantiated the charge. And no one who looks closely into current sentiment and current modes of living and measuring life can fail to see what I say. It astonishes me sometimes so much, that I forget what century I am living in—under what system of thought and life. It looks now and then so much as if Christ's coming had been a dream, and one were only half-awake to the fact of its being a dream. For when the claims of Christianity are put forward, when the kind of life which it insists on is insisted on as a matter of moment, and an endeavour made to have it translated into act and fact in the life of each of us, in our sentiments and thoughts, in our personal behaviour, in our behaviour to those we have to meet, in our commercial dealings—when men are asked to work by its rule, to keep houses on its model, to build houses as it indicates, to buy and sell as it teaches, to carry on government after its idea—when these things are suggested, you know the reply: "We cannot. The thing is not possible. We must do as we may, not as we should. We cannot unhinge this admirably arranged system, under which we lead a tolerable existence, for the sake of introducing what, of course, we greatly admire and sympathize with." Exactly as the young man, we should like, or think we should like, eternal life; and remember what we found out once this life to be—not an inheritance that men would fall heirs to after the conclusion of the life here. That is not the New Testament eternal life, nor Christ's. The eternal life is quality of life, and not duration. There is no contention in the New Testament about the latter, and the contention of religion, when religion is rightly apprehended, is not about duration of life, but kind of life, the life of a man as it was in Jesus—a life here—a life which you must lead in your heart, follow out in your homes and pursue in your business, display in your governments, in whatever hand is put to or mind engaged in. And what about it elsewhere? I would much rather see a healthy and rational interest in the eternal life here than elsewhere; and when we have it here, it will be time enough to inquire about it elsewhere, and we shall then be better able to make the inquiry. I heard a man the other day quote the opinion of an old writer with reference to the future life of animals, and it was something like this—that they were so badly used by man, sometimes thoughtlessly, sometimes with thought, that there must be a future to give them compensation— an existence when all their wrongs would be righted. The same argument, you know, has been used to support the belief in a future for man. The inequalities and injustices here are so great, that there must be a settling day and a recompense. I could not help whispering to my nearest neighbour, that we should take good care to prevent any need for compensation hereafter. What is the use of dwelling on that prospect either for men or animals? Here make the eternal life to be felt, which is a power, as you know it in Christ, to adjust inequalities, to right wrongs, to obviate the need of compensation afterwards, through the active and intelligent exercise of Christian love. "Thou hast given him power . . . that he should give eternal life to as many as Thou hast given him;" "Whoso eateth my flesh and drinketh my blood (I have explained this symbolism to you before) hath eternal life;" and many another saying which I might give you, many an act which I might recal to you. The interview with the young man shows what both Christ and the youth thought about eternal life; the question, "What shall I do to have it?" and most definitely the answer, telling us clearly and distinctly what it consists in—in a quality of heart and inward disposition that finds expression for itself in the whole conduct and business of life. We like, I say, or think we should like, precisely as the young man, this eternal life. We often find, as he discovered, that we like something else vastly better. We may make the discovery with sorrow, but, with it or without it, it is a common experience that we prefer—I do not say possessions, as he did; we prefer what we have—the way we live, the way the world wags in, the life the world leads and encourages us to live: we prefer this, I say, to the eternal life, when it comes plainly and absolutely to a choice. Now I say this with no reference to contrasts that are sometimes drawn. I do not say that we reject faith in Christ, nor that we refuse the way of salvation, nor that we will not come to the Cross—because I know perfectly well that there is no use holding this language. These are generalities that we can all escape from, and not be made feel that we are anything else than good Christians. I say broadly and fully, and in the language of common life and of human experience, and I can appeal to the sense and observation of every one in saying it, that we refuse the Christian standard of morality. I am not going to deny for a moment that we have no display of Christian love—no trace anywhere of the influence of Christian sentiment. You would show me Infirmaries, Convalescent Homes, Sailors' Homes, Industrial Institutions, Hospitals, Poor-houses, Missions. I have seen them all, and thought about them all, and am ready to admire what is good in them. I do not see what we could do without them. I think they deserve all the sympathy and support we give to them, and more, if we can possibly give more. But these are not the best nor the truest illustrations of Christian morality. I am of opinion that a great many such things will disappear when Christian morals are in force among us. Some of these are there, not because of our adherence to Christian morals, but because of the absence of active and energetic Christian morality. "Love erects and maintains them." True, my friends; but the want of a Christ's love in the first place necessitates, I occasionally think, the building and maintenance of some of them.

We feel untouched on the rehearsal of the prohibitive commandments; and if there be any others prohibitive, likely enough the great bulk of the Christian world would remain untouched on hearing them. "All these we have kept—what more do you want?" I want that which is everywhere lacking, which everybody sees is lacking, which few indeed have moral courage to supply—the straightforward reduction to life and the business of life of the religion universally professed among us. We may be pleased with our attainments in this respect. We are mostly very well pleased with these, and think the Gospel perhaps might be preached with some advantage in "lands" very nearly adjoining our church. I can tell you quite soberly that the Gospel has very urgent need to penetrate very respectable houses, and find its way into most reputable breasts, and leaven lives that are by many considered to be patterns of goodness. And I repeat again, I do not disparage their goodness—only let it be understood that it is not always Christian goodness. None of you suppose, I hope, that when Jesus appeared in Palestine, the country was a sink of iniquity—that it was any worse than our own is at present. I have never found any evidence to show that the country had not a great many patterns of goodness; and, so far as I have been able to learn, there were not the horrible instances which our modern towns supply of the other side of life. His contention was not with the class of men and women who had fallen below the level of the current standard of morals. I think we have the best reasons for concluding that he gave these people all the help and healing that lay in a nature like his to give. But so far as the authentic histories of his teaching are to be our guides, his labour was to a large extent directed to another quarter. And what quarter do you suppose? Do we not base our work among the outcast and degraded—the little we do—I say the little we do, for I hold that we do next to nothing, and when we do ever so little, we think a great deal of it—do we not base the little we do in the slums, upon what Jesus did—upon the principles he has given us? That is the case, and there is truth in the ground claimed for action of this kind. I do not think this case can be too strongly put; and without doubt it is not felt in anything like its real strength. But in so putting matters, do not let us overlook a most important and most prominent part of the campaign, if I may so say, of Christ. For it very much resembled that, and for moral and spiritual power we have nothing like it in Christianity. And in what quarter, I ask again, was this great moral campaign carried on? Was it not in a great degree—in the greatest degree, as it seems sometimes—among what we call the patterns of goodness? Did he not deal, and think it one of the first and foremost parts of his work to deal, with men who not only kept the commandments, but in their scrupulousness went beyond the commandments? I have said before to you, that these were not what we call bad men—irreligious men—they were what I occasionally describe to you as "the good and careful men of the villages," who, while they seem so good, are the real pilferers of a high and healthy virtue—they were the religious and respectable classes in the country. And very much of what has come down to us as authentic words of Christ's, are words of warning and rebuke addressed to these classes —to men, observe you, who came up to the standard that many of us are aiming at, and would be content to see reached—to the prohibitive moral ideal of Judaism, to a negative goodness, of which the best that we can say is, that it does not do this and that—it does not kill, it does not steal, it does not drink, it does not commit adultery. That is something to say; but with Christianity before Europe for nineteen hundred years, and with its ideal constantly held up to ourselves, its significance is very much diminished. This prohibitive form of morality is an early and preliminary stage of it. Christianity is an advance on this, a movement of a most distinct kind from a simple negative goodness to positive—from the strength that lies " in sitting still," which we read about to-day in our Old Testament lesson (religiously we are very strong in that), to the aggressive divine force of a Christ. We do not quite realize as we should where we are in the world's history; we do not feel in all their force the demands that Christianity makes upon us, the peculiar character of its morality, and the quite determinative life and conduct it exacts from its followers in every affair in life. And when I say we do not feel these demands, I mean the great body of the well-doing part of our communities. Compare in your minds for one moment the inner truth of the Christian scheme with the outward morality of modern life in the phases of it that pass for good, and you will agree with me that the Gospel or message of Christ is needed in quarters where we sometimes think it an impertinence—every bit as much required as it was by the higher and middle classes in Jerusalem. There is not brought against these classes any charge of what we call viciousness. It is not said by Christ that they infringed any of the negative commandments which we would like to see adopted as the common standard of virtue—which we have chosen as the standard. We have no hint of any such thing. They were moral and virtuous after the manner of the Decalogue. They refrained from this and that, and it was this morally inactive state, leading in Christ's view and in the religious view to forms of absolute immorality and wrong, that was the evil of his time; and it is the one terrible evil in our time. Much in the other evils that we see and deplore is traceable to this; much in them, at all events, would be removed and ameliorated had we a genuine conversion of our middle and upper classes to the simple and straightforward religion of Jesus —to the religion, with a text like this before us, which I may call the religion of humanity. That religion is not one of mere moral restraint—of prohibition. It has left that stage of life behind. I shall not trouble you by showing you to-night where and how this advance of Christianity on Judaism comes about. It is sufficient for my purpose that it has come about; that we cannot deny it; that we are under a system which says, Thou shalt positively do this, and not one that says, Thou shalt not do this and that; that the law—I do not say of religion—but that the law of human life and society is no longer obedience to the statutory precepts of Judaism—abstention from certain lines of conduct—but submission to a precept which renders all statutes nugatory, and whose fulfilment lies in action, not in abstinence or inaction, in what we know as Christian love, in an active and generous and intelligent furtherance of the good of others. As you know, much of what I have called statutory morality is only a furtherance of our own private and individual good, and our own good in the lowest sense of that word. It does not mean the upraising of our spirit to the Divine Spirit, the filling of our souls with the Divine goodness, but very often the mere warding off of the material distress of life. We have missed the salient feature of our religion, and we are very well pleased to miss it, as it would seem. There are increasing numbers who are very ready to tithe what is hardly worth tithing, and which yields little for the real work and end of establishing and extending Christ's kingdom, if only they are let alone with regard to the main item. Do not let us suppose, what I believe we all suppose, that the better people among us are superior to the men against whom this very kind of procedure was urged nineteen hundred years ago. We are not better. The influential classes among us—and I say with regret what I have felt for years and never said—the influential classes and people of repute, and people of what is called good and honest behaviour, are not in Christ's meaning fulfilling the law. I look in vain, in the decorum that characterizes them, for any earnest attempt to give force to the one point which is the test point in the law, as Christ has made us understand it. Love is more than Paul says in his cautious argument; it does more than merely work no ill to a neighbour; it transcends the law, and worketh every conceivable good.

I must guard myself before I close from one misconception of my remarks. Some of you may go away with the idea that I want your money for your neighbours. I shall not wholly deny that, but that was not once in my mind; and I begin to see quite distinctly that if people only fulfilled the law, as we now know it, in their positions in life, love to our neighbours would not have to take this shape so often as it does; and when it had to do so, it would be less with the feeling that we were doing something beyond and above the requirement of the law. You never can exceed its requirement. The low and quite trifling claims upon us, that I have just hinted at, for money, are, in many cases, due to ourselves and those like us, and are in reality fruits of the great neglect of the one vital doctrine in religion in our social and industrial life.

XI.

14th December, 1879.
Evening Service.

John xvii. 23.—"That they may be one, even as we are one."

I said last Sunday night that we missed the salient points in the Christian religion, and were seemingly tolerably well content to do it.[1] I mentioned one of these, which I hold, from the express words of our Founder and his life, to be, what I called, the test of a religious life—the vital doctrine in Christianity—without which, in other words, Christianity has no meaning—without which, in our daily life and work, we are ourselves, as Paul saw, also without sense or meaning—religiously speaking, we are nothing. I am not to-night to enter again upon that subject, although it will bear enlarging upon—and, in fact, fully and faithfully enlarged upon, would cover everything that I have to say from this place. For love embraceth the law, and the law, as our New Testament represents it, is the sum of all Christian instruction. But there is one remark I desire to make with reference to it. Love is of much greater sweep than we often think it is. It is a principle that we are to take with us everywhere, and everywhere to apply. It is not to be kept for your private and domestic life, but for the whole of life—for your public

[1] Sermon X.

and business life. You are to have it in your heart, not merely—to take a contrasted example—when you build a house for yourself and those dear to you, but when you build for those whom Jesus calls your neighbours, who should also be dear to you. And, I think, if we had love of this kind—if we had religion of this colour—we should have, what I incidentally said last week, less need for some of the forms of it which we at present look upon as peculiar evidence of the existence of Christian love. The want among us of a neighbourly Christian love like this, has, I may say without being charged with any extravagance, worked a great deal of ill to our neighbours. I do not see yet any direct tendency to work for their good by rightly using means of this description. "We cannot," it is said again. "We cannot," is a very serious confession in this connection, and is no less than this, "We cannot be Christian"—that, in the only way in which we can really and effectually exhibit Christian love to our neighbours, we are helpless. And so, out of Christian love, we tithe ourselves a little for the maintenance of Christian institutions, and console ourselves with the reflection, that in business we are to practise strictly business principles, and keep the religious department stringently isolated. That is what I called tithing trifles and overlooking the main item—a practice by no means confined to Scribes and Pharisees. I read not long ago in the works of a very keen observer, in speaking of the class of virtues that are brought into play for the carrying on of the business of the world, words somewhat like the following: These virtues are not to be exclusively practised by one class of men, while the religious virtues of heroism and holiness are practised by another. He had, he said, a great respect, as everybody of sense has, for the practical and prudential virtues of life, as we call them; but this partition of the life of man did not, in his estimation, enhance the working virtues. Now I do not think that it is exactly as this writer supposes. We never think there must be two classes of men—one practising prudence, and being skilled in affairs—another practising holiness and heroism, and being—well, we usually say—muddlers. On the contrary, each man tries a little of both—and, what I wish to note is, tries to keep the one clear of the other—in their proper sphere. That is the seat of the mischief among us. It is here we miss the real point in Christianity. I have given you one illustration, but that, you all are aware, is on the same footing with others that I might give—others which your own business experience will supply to you. For the building of houses is carried on, on exactly the same principles as the manufacture of jute or anything else. Now, our religion opposes this mode of keeping the virtues apart. You are especially to see that you take your heroism and holiness to your mills and shops and offices. You will find in these places a magnificent field for the exercise of them—a field mostly unbroken. Our present plan of confining the exercise of these virtues to some private and particular walk of life, has nearly extinguished them. These different qualities are not, as the man I alluded to says, to be assigned to different kinds of men; nor are they, as is often the case, to be pursued by the same man at different times or in distinct acts in life. Heroism and holiness are to work along with prudence in conducting the ordinary business of life. Christian men, if they are to be Christian men—that is, having wholeness and roundness of nature—and not simply ingenious pieces of mechanism, must call in

Christ's love to execute their work—to determine their relation to their customers, to their work-people, to all with whom they may be brought into connection—they must call in this as well as shrewdness. It is not within the line of my remarks, otherwise I could show you what unnatural and contradictory characters have been produced among us through the artificial separation of the religious and the trade principle. We cut ourselves in two. This half is to do business with as little as possible reference to that. That half is destined for the exercise of Christian love, and is to work, as much as possible, clear of the other. That is not Christianity. Christianity is to be made tell— and it can only effectually be made tell—Christianity is to be made tell upon the world by being brought to bear with full force upon every division of life and labour. Christian love is an absolutely necessary factor in political economy, and in the whole affairs of society; and by no means to be practised as a luxury in certain private and irregular ways. This is the conversion that I said we needed.

But here in my text again I meet with a matter that is not maintained by Christian people as it should be; nor understood by them, nor appreciated as it deserves. I have chosen it for two reasons. Because it is beyond doubt what I have called a salient point in Christianity: and it is also, as we shall see, not by any means distantly related to the subject we have just been considering. Union is, taking our New Testament and its teachers again as our guides— union is an essential in Christianity. It is merely the outward expression of its spirit of love. The example which Jesus gives us shows this—" That they may be one, even as we are one." There is no need for me to take you into the curious opinions which have been held about this oneness between God and Christ, founded upon sayings like this and others, that declare, "I and my Father are one." The immediate meaning is quite plain. It is a religious and moral one. The curious opinions to which I refer, and which culminated in the doctrine of the Trinity, are based on a metaphysical meaning, and are not without great interest, I assure you. But the oneness which Christ showed so much anxiety for, was not a oneness of this kind. It has sense for us only in the oneness that must have struck any intelligent hearer of his—oneness in spirit, and purpose, and aim. As I am like my Father, doing the works my Father does, continually speaking the words my Father speaks, displaying the love that is in the heart of Infinite Love, and so manifesting his name and character to the world—as I do this, and may be said to be one with him—working for the accomplishment of his designs—expressing his thoughts for the world—so, O Father, may these be one! As my spirit and my will are so through and through permeated with thine, that my will is thy will, and thine, mine—thy thoughts for man, my thoughts—thy workings for his salvation and elevation, my own and only work, so that between thee and me there is no division, but the deepest union and harmony in soul and intent, compared with which other unions are mere junctions and amalgamations—this, in truth, oneness, identity in the root and essence of being,—as there is this between thee and me, so may they be one like us, cherishing the same purpose, devoted to the same cause, inspired by the same love, moving to the great end, step by step with thee, whither thou art leading man.

A great and noble thought, you must allow. A fundamental and root-conception in Christianity, intimately related to the principle of love—an idea both grand and good, having in it the very odour of the soul of Jesus; and for the sake of things that stink in all souls like his, for the sake of ideas that are altogether paltry and contemptible, Christendom has given up the conception of its Master, and, what looks as if it were wantonly done, obliterated the very feature, as I showed you one day, by which the world was to know that Christians knew Christ, and through which the world was itself to become acquainted with him. We may think this a small matter. Evidently the Christian world is of that opinion. We may suppose that it is a subject on which various views may be held, and quite secondary. To any one who knows Christ's mind, and has the slightest acquaintance with Christian truth, it is a great matter, part of the greatest matter—not secondary at all, but in the fore-front in religion—not a question at all for various views, but one on which there is no possibility for variety of opinion. We see Christianity split up now into so many sections, that we think the division quite a normal thing, and you will find people ready to go on splitting and dividing. You will also find many ready with their reasons for such a state in the Christian world. You never saw yet any condition of things, but you would find men ready to give reasons why they should be so. But within the circle of Christian truth and principles, there is no reason worth looking at that can excuse the present aspect of the Christian community in the face of the world—no reason, I mean, that is not at the same time a giving up of what is fundamental in Christian thought. As love is to be the one mark of a Christian soul, the "note" by which a soul can tell that it is in union with God and Jesus—love carried over your whole converse and business in the world—so is union of such souls the open testimony to the world of this inward oneness. And, I may say, in proportion as you have the inward oneness, you have the union I speak of. What the present state of Christianity announces is not the harmony of its individual members on the great principle of their religion. It speaks very positively of a quite different state of mind—of a very profound indifference to the great principle of Jesus and his kingdom, and of a foolish and obstinate perseverance in matters hardly at all connected with that kingdom—I should say, not in the least connected with that kingdom, but most determinedly opposed to it. What is connected with it, inevitably leads to union, and union of no external kind; but union, like Christ's with God—soul union—melting of heart and purpose on the great purpose—burning up in the ardour of divine love all mean and petty jealousies. I know nothing—and I say nothing with full consciousness of what has divided what we call Christendom—I know nothing that might not be buried in a grave from which there would be no rising, did Christian men and women feel, with its true force, the supreme and only aim of Jesus. The weakness of our perception there is the measure of our capacity for discerning differences that religiously are of no moment, and is also the measure of our readiness to join on these differences. And on the other side, I find—to the paralysis of all effort for good in towns at all adequate to the state of the case—I find, on the other hand, that a readiness to join on differences that, compared with the supreme aim, are worthless—not even worth the stone and lime spent on them—is a very correct measure of our disregard of the only purpose which I am aware Jesus had in his mind. It is perfectly deplorable. To any one who has faith in Christianity, nothing could well be more deplorable. Its fundamental ideas, and its distinct aims, its most vital doctrines, are overlooked and neglected in a way no one would believe, unless he fairly and frankly confronted our times with New Testament truth. I am talking generalities? I can be special, my friends; I can be very special. I have said before that Christianity was a social reformation on a somewhat extensive scale. I wish any Christian man to tell me what our Christian churches are doing towards this social reformation—what effort they are making to introduce into our life some of the things that Jesus endeavoured to introduce. What might not be done in a town like ours to bring, what I once was at pains to describe to you as salvation, to the men and women in it, if churches and their adherents were at one with Jesus on this matter, which is the matter in religion, and not at loggerheads with each other on matters of less than no concern by comparison? I know forms of unbelief that pious people are amazed at. In the bosom of piety itself, there is this form of unbelief and irreligion, which I cannot match anywhere—not even in the ranks of infidelity. I have often wished that something might be done among us on a scale somewhat commensurate with the human love that one supposes to be in minds united to Jesus and his purposes, and also sufficient to meet the needs of our community; and I find—I may as well say it —Christian love ice-bound. "We have agencies"—some of these I named last Sunday. We should be ashamed of ourselves! We know they are not sufficient—that they are wretchedly inadequate—that they hardly touch the rim of the evil. Every Christian man knows it; every Christian community knows it; and every Christian community is satisfied with the knowledge of it. What idea we form of religion, and of the Founder of ours in particular, passes my comprehension altogether. Under what image, or if under any, we carry in our hearts the memory of the Man of love and sorrow—the picture of his life—is more than I can tell. I have heard of a great many difficulties and puzzles in connection with religion, but all the intellectual and logical puzzles in this connection may be taken at one bite—this absolute contradiction in the very life of religion —the worship of Christ—which is nothing less than reverence to his spirit—his principles—his manner of fulfilling life's duties—prostration of the man in us to the man in Jesus—the contradiction in religious life itself—of worship such as I describe, and fact such as we have it in divided Christendom, is quite irreconcilable. Division as division would not trouble me greatly. It is what the division signifies, and the substantial work it hinders, that are to me the serious aspects of present Christianity. The signification, as I have hinted, is, that we think more of conceits of our own which have nothing whatever to do with the stern realities of human life, and can contribute nothing to the carrying out of the divine purposes, and push aside the one question that has to do with these grave realities, and is an essential in the evolving plan of the world. There is no fancy in this. It is a most lamentable fact, and until we awaken to the calamity involved in such a fact, the progress of Christian thought and feeling, in spite of growing churches, and, I should say also, occasionally because of growing churches, is positively barred. I shall never believe—and no one acquainted with their Bible can believe —that the world, calling itself Christian at present, knows intelligently what Christianity is, so long as it shows that it has no perception of what it can join together on—of what, if it is in the mind of Christ, it ought to join together on—of what, if its worship of him were, what I said just now, profound recognition by our nature of his manner of life—would make every Christian soul fly together and unite in one act, and with one spirit and will. But we worship, I am sorry to say it, very often our own nostrums, and not the idea of Jesus. And the clear perception of this idea, as the uniting force of all true admirers of Christ, is thrown into the background, and we have amalgamated societies for maintaining notions which, I will venture to say, are so far irreligious as they conceal the main Christian conception, and delay the certain result of a pure and genuine religion. That sure result is oneness. Don't let the present look of things mislead you. No man imbued with the simple religious idea can be disunited from another similarly imbued. What keeps them apart is defect in their perception of the religious idea—a certain element, therefore, of irreligion—in this case a very considerable element. What keeps nations apart, and has always been most powerful in estranging them, is not the idea of humanity, but imperfect perception of this idea—in plain words, a certain element which we call inhumanity. The compass and depth of this union of races is a true measure of the hold which this idea has upon the peoples of the world. And it is the same with religion. The falling away from union, and the persistence in this falling away, are the truest measures you could have of the obscurity in the minds of religious people of the religious idea—of the weak hold they have of the great thought of Christianity. We should push for what Christ prays, and give up pushing for what there has been so much push in the history of

Christianity. And when I counsel you to this, I must request you to notice, that I am not advising it for the mere sake of what is called a union or organization in Christendom after any patterns we have. That is not my intention at all. I am perhaps, if anything, a little too indifferent about organizations. I counsel this on the pure ground of religion—as an essential in the Christian religion—as something, without which we cannot be said to be Christian. It is, any one can see who knows much about history—and it is a great misfortune in our time that men who lead, and those who are led, do not know it in the inner movements of it—it is a poor thing to push for some matters that are being sought for by Christian people—matters that, in the very nature of the case, do not promote union. If these things, scaled by duly qualified men, outweigh the purpose of Jesus, let us have them by all means. Let the purpose of Christ stand postponed. But what are any of these questions, or all of them, compared with this purpose which all Christians are said to worship—if they worship at all? You might throw every one of them to the winds, and be none the worse, but a great deal the better, for being rid of them. Christianity is a social power. We stand apart on ground quite away from what is strictly religious. We hesitate to join in one effort on what alone is Christian and religious—with the heart and spirit and temper of a Christ—at one with him, and with the Spirit of the universe, and with all good souls, to work together simply for good—for good among our fellow-townsmen. I seek nothing out of the way—nothing quixotic. I am aiming at something strictly practical—something that will not tax your pockets nor your energies—something that will save the pockets and energies of a few wild people who make vain efforts single-handed in the direction I speak of, but the work can never be done single-handed. A Christ could not alone accomplish what he set for himself. We need many Christs—Christians I always call Christs, and shall continue to hope that some day soon they will justify their name. And why should the work he came to do be allowed to slacken with so many nominal hands? When I consider that possibly in this town, which, like others, cannot face its poverty, its misery, its ignorance, its vice—which feels itself quite helpless to deal with them—which weeps at the sight of it all, and gives a crust here and a penny there, a pair of shoes and an old coat—when I consider that here there are probably fifty large and small societies with thousands of adherents to the divinest and most intelligible form of humanity and philanthropy, and that it stands helpless before the small task at its doors, what am I to conclude? One of two things. Either we are grossly ignorant of our religion, or quite indifferent to the one way in which it can be carried out. "We cannot cope with the evil." The statement will not bear looking at. We have never tried to cope with it. What is to hinder—if intelligence and Christian sympathy are set to work throughout this town in a union purely religious—what is to hinder the whole town from being divided, and work of the lightest and easiest description allotted to Christian men and women? Nothing, that I can see, but the indifference of the Christian communities, their want of union on what alone is essential to Christianity, and, what I have called, their ice-bound feelings. There is no Christian man who has deep at heart the good of his fellows, rather than the benefit and furtherance of his church or whim of any kind, but has wished, above all wishes, for a realization of Christ's prayer, and that the walls of churches should be broken down, and acknowledged and substantial co-operation of each with each begun. I do not here point at that paltry kind of good feeling between churches which newspapers clap their hands at, when a man of one denomination preaches in the pulpit of another denomination; that only shows the depth and density of popular ignorance all through this whole matter. The present state of things is an offence to all Christian feeling—a blot on religion. People say, divisions are needed—that they are useful in exciting rivalry. The argument is too weak to be noticed. Division in religion is largely opportunity to pursue and peddle at a crotchet, to cultivate conceit and the most horrible form of foppery, religious foppery. When I think sometimes of the enormous machinery, and good ability, and great means, employed in these various divisions, purely for the support of what has created division, I cannot help wishing that they were devoted for ten years to the carrying on, with as much zeal, of legitimate Christian work, and work that should and would unite Christendom were it seriously taken in hand.

XII.

11TH JANUARY, 1880.
Morning Service.

COLOSSIANS iii. 24.—"Ye serve the Master, Christ."

THIS is merely keeping to the translation made in the first verse of the next chapter, and which, it appears to me, gives the meaning of the writer. And in the verse before the text you can make the same alteration: "Whatsoever ye do, do it from the soul—spiritedly—as to the Master . . . knowing that of the Master ye shall receive the reward." It has been often remarked, and, in my opinion, with considerable truth, that the church, or the religious community in its teaching capacity, has dealt too little with the affairs of life. It has occupied itself with questions that are remote, very remote indeed, from what touches the men and women who listen to its teaching. It is with great regret, I assure you, that I feel I have to make this acknowledgment; but the fact has been too patent, and the evil—for I cannot regard it as anything short of a pernicious evil—too widespread to be concealed. It is right that the fact should be stated, that the evil should be openly confessed. If we saw it—I mean if Christian people saw it—clearly, we might hope for a very speedy amendment. Other people see it, and although they make the most of it, I am rather thankful to them than otherwise for making so much of it. A very able writer—one of the ablest and most popular writers of the day—says in the bitterness of his spirit, and with bare justice, that "men who profess Christianity and practise Paganism feel no sympathy with an earnest belief that a rationalized version of the ethical principles of Christianity will eventually be acted upon;" that "men who lament the spreading disbelief in eternal damnation are not in sympathy with such a belief;" that "from the ten thousand priests of the religion of love who are silent when the nation is moved by the religion of hate, will come no sign of assent."[1] That is very strong language, my friends, and especially strong occurring where it does occur, on the deliberate and sober pages of a philosophical treatise. I am not sorry for the words, nor angry even, although I may be roughly thrown among the ten thousand priests of love who calmly behold a religion of hate. There is truth in the description, if it is vehemently stated. I have myself made an effort to say the same thing more moderately with reference to matters nearer your doors and mine than Afghan and Africa are. I have a very strong feeling that we shall never treat strange people well, and in the spirit of our religion, until we learn first to treat our own people as Christ has told us. While we have among us, in such nakedness that sometimes makes me ashamed, the kind of policy and conduct and sentiment that exist, the policy of our nation to subject races, to which this writer no doubt refers, must be what it is. And it is what it is, my friends, not for the first time, it grieves me painfully to say. When our doings, for the last century or more, in the different quarters of the world where our

[1] Spencer, "The Data of Ethics."

people have wandered, are recorded by an impartial historian—which, depend upon it, will be the case some day—we shall have much to abate our pride, and make us speak more softly of Providence and the Saxon race. I have myself accumulated authenticated facts enough to make me burn with shame at the mention of our colonization of America, Australia, New Zealand. We have all heard of the doings of the Spaniards on the American continent, but we can nearly match them. Only there is this difference, that the brilliant material success of our settlements has in the mean time nearly eclipsed transactions of a moral kind which will yet throw a terrible shadow on that success. But they are recorded—never fear that; and if they were not, they have left, one can see, as all action does, their indelible mark upon our national sentiment and thought. There is that much truth, then, we must allow, in religion and its teaching as related to the affairs of life. But I would desire you to note well that it is not, as has been observed in the words I quoted to you, confined to men who lament the widespread disbelief in eternal damnation. I suspect, when you look into it, neglect of what I speak of is quite as much, and perhaps more—I shall not apportion blame—at the door of those who have made efforts to spread this disbelief. It is, in truth, the fatal mistake of both sides of controversies like these—and I mention this one because it has already been suggested to me as a distinctive one—it is the fatal mistake, I repeat, of both sides that they have made so much as they have done of matters of this kind. Where, let me ask, is there authority for identifying these questions in one way or another with the Christian religion?—of so identifying them, at least, to the extent, on any side, as to make of them important and essential religious truths, to the exclusion very often from the minds of people, who are tickled with questions of this nature, of truths that are essentially religious? I do not think that it is unimportant what we may think about eternal salvation or the reverse—what we may think about other matters that have been discussed among us. I am of opinion that it is extremely advisable to have wise and discreet, reasonable and true notions of these matters, just as it is advisable that we entertain the same kind of notions about everything that our minds occupy themselves with. I think every educated man ought to hold himself ready to bring this about. But these are questions which have to do with culture, general education and enlightenment, and must be worked out on these lines and with these appliances, and not on purely religious grounds and with religious apparatus. They are not, to speak strictly, religious questions; and to disturb religious feeling in regard to them is not only mischievous, but wholly unwarrantable. You are not pleased with the view about the Scriptures commonly entertained? Well, what as a teacher are you to do? Hammer away at the vulgar notion until it and the contents of Scripture are completely knocked out of people's heads? I think, with all deference, that a more rational course and a manlier is, whatever opinions are current, to fix the attention of earnest men upon the matter of these books—to get them to attend to that, to understand that—if possible, to get them to accept that, and never mind much in the interval how this matter came to be there. When I read to you last Sunday morning the outpourings of men's souls long ago in their hours of trial and calamity, what man among you thought for a moment of how these soul-moving words came there? What is it to the matter we then heard how they came? They are true and human words, and, on any supposition as to their origin, across all these centuries still touch our hearts and answer to our deepest feelings.[1] I shall suppose a case. Suppose you found in a walk some leaves on which were printed the justest thoughts, most tender and exquisite feelings, pure aspirations, sentiments that lifted you out of yourself, everything that in literature is refining and ennobling—would you refuse to have to do with the matter that was so excellent, because you could not come to any conclusion as to the authorship and conditions of composition of the literary treasure? You would be curious to know these things. I should not think much of you if you were not; but I should think nothing at all of you if the inability to settle these, prevented your mastering the contents and assimilating the beauty and excellence of the writing. Suppose you were told that the book had dropped from the clouds, would that make its truths truer? Or suppose you were asked to believe that it was in its origin the same as other books, would that make its beauty less beautiful, its thoughts less just? Would you think it reasonable in any case to put the book in good binding and with a good clasp, and to keep it practically closed until you had come to some determinate understanding about how it was written and how it came to be there? And when I ask again for our warranty in doing in religion as we have done, I can find none. There is nothing in our religious literature to match what we have done, and there is nothing of the sort in any earnest primitive religious literature. Religious men were always engaged upon human problems. My text is an

---

[1] This refers to a selection of passages from the Scriptures, read in place of a sermon the Sunday after the Tay-bridge disaster.

example of this, and only one example among thousands.
To find a text for what I have called the remoter problems
is a difficult thing, and strictly, I believe, an impossible
thing. I know the difficulty, and am speaking from experience, for I have occasionally to speak about these questions, and any text a man may choose for this purpose
requires always a very free and liberal treatment. It is
quite otherwise when you keep to what our religious
writers saw to be the matter in religion—that is, our life in
the world under the manifold aspects of it. This is spoken
of directly on every page and in every paragraph. And it is
only when we touch this that we come upon what is essentially the religious problem. That problem is not belief or
disbelief in eternal damnation. It would do us some good
to leave that matter on one side—a matter not religious, or,
at least, seldom religiously treated. In the voluminous
speaking about it, how much goes beyond, or even comes
up to, what Christ said to the lawyer who asked him a
question on this subject? The lawyer, you remember, gave
his reading of the law in these words: "Thou shalt love
the Lord thy God with all thy heart, and with all thy soul
(or spiritedly) .... and thy neighbour as thyself;" and
Christ answered, "This do and thou shalt live." Without
this—if with absolute correctness any one can be said to
be without this—Jesus, neither eternally nor temporarily,
would admit life to man; for with him, and in the right
sense of human existence, it is only as we live in God and
in His love that we live at all. And it is to draw our
attention to this fact that all religious men have put out
their strength, precisely as in my text here. Ye workers and
labourers in the world, it is not with the matters that your

ears may have sometimes itched after—not about yes or no
in regard to what is called eternal damnation—not about
yes or no as to the sacred authorship of your religious books
—but about the spirit of your work and the principles of
your life—the feelings in your heart—the temper of your
mind—these it is that are the truly damning things or
saving things for you. Religion, in the only right accepta-
tion of it, is the most pertinent thing to the life of each of
us; to a community such as ours it has a most direct and
especial message, as indeed it has to every community. It
intermeddles with all our affairs. Wherever men are, it has
something to say to them, and something that is absolutely
necessary they should listen to. As it has been dealt with
and taught, we have begun to imagine that it was about the
last thing we had to keep in mind. If it were taught as it
ought to be, men would see that it is the very first thing
they have to do with;—that, in Christ's words, as they have
or have not to do with it, so do men live or not live; as
you work by it or do not work by it, so is your work fruit-
ful and permanent, or it is fruitless and vain. That I say,
not as uttering a general sentiment which will be approved
of by spiritual and religious men—I say it as a well-authen-
ticated fact in history, a fact which men and nations in the
past preach to us as loudly and plainly as any teacher in
the Old and New Testaments. "Love the Lord thy God
with all thy heart and soul, and thy neighbour as thyself,
and thou shalt live"—do the other thing, and thou shalt
die—these are no mere words of Christ's, no mere ideal
sentiment; they are blazoned on the annals of every country, and may be deciphered in the history of every soul.

It is a simple historical fact with a very fine and impressive setting, but not nearly so imposing as the many facts themselves, when the writer in Daniel makes Belteshazzar read this writing—"Thou art weighed!" "The God in whose hand thy breath is, and whose are all thy works, hast thou not glorified!" Visionary religious poetry! No, my friends, but very matter-of-fact reading of life: Christ in the Old Testament; religion and the religious life at the base of everything that will bear the brunt of trial. For every man of us, and every piece of work of ours, must be put to the test, in order to see the stuff that it is made of. My dear friends, we are all fallen into gross and palpable delusions. Ostensibly we spin thread and weave cloth and shape wood and iron, and busy ourselves in a great many ways, and we ask, What has religion to do with these things? Avowedly we do all these to make money. That is the delusion. In reality these are phantasms only—the reality will come clearly out some day, and does show itself occasionally to most people, if they would take time to look —in reality, we are all this time shaping souls, weaving at the "roaring loom of time" the delicate texture of the man within. Spinning! Yes—the thread which Clotho is fabled to have spun, but which is our own work. To amass wealth! Yes—but not the wealth we all think about when we hear these words. Do not suppose that I despise the means of living—that were to defeat life; but do not let us—which is a much more likely thing now-a-days—do not let any man suppose for one single moment that having the means he has the life, or that the means is for an instant to be put in the scale with the life itself—that being destitute of means is to be placed side by side in your imagination with an impoverished spirit. We labour to amass wealth, but wealth that no banker can take charge of, that you cannot leave behind to friends, but that, be it much or little, is inseparable from the mind and memory of your mysterious personality. All work that is not in reality of this kind is most laborious indolence merely. And I say so although you may tell me that half the world carries its potatoes and corn and gunpowder in your sacks—that you can withstand unprecedented years of distress. This is not the only outcome, nor the chief outcome, of work by men in this world, nor the final test of its worth, as we all know. What is it to help people to potatoes and powder if our own souls should be dying of hunger? It is no satisfaction to a man that he has sent so many miles of shirting and broadcloth to cover naked backs, if he has not learnt how to clothe his spirit in the process—nothing to have built houses against the weather, and to find, when the earthly house of this tabernacle is dissolved, that our life within is without the only shelter possible for it, the "house not made with hands," the palace of pure thoughts, gentle affections, kindly impulses, which hedge in all good and tender souls.

I only wish to remind you in these words of what we all forget, that, whatever we work at, it is the Master, Christ, we serve; that there is not a stroke struck here in this busy town, not a transaction made, but, if it is well and wisely done, is done to him. If it is not done to him, if it cannot be done to him—it may be large, it may be prosperous—we may as well leave it alone. This is how men who knew what religion was, looked upon it—not as a matter of debate and doubt and inquiry, but, like life itself, a matter for action. I have said that our work is without value apart from religion, and our religion is something worse than valueless away from our work. We must begin at least to learn that we have to look for it, not so much where we have been in the habit of doing so, but in our mills, and shops of all kinds, and offices. My friends, one cannot but wonder how differently the world would be served, did we all in the first place, and with the simplest sincerity, "serve the Master; Christ."

XIII.

1ST FEBRUARY, 1880.
Morning Service.

ISAIAH liii. 4, 5.—"Surely he hath borne our griefs and carried our sorrows: yet we did esteem him stricken, smitten of God and afflicted. But he was wounded for our transgressions; he was bruised for our iniquities; the chastisement of our peace was upon him; and with his stripes we are healed."

THERE have been two interpretations of this chapter, one of the grandest, I hold, among many noble passages in the most remarkable book which we possess. One interpretation sees in it a prophetic account of the life and sufferings of Jesus, and a proof of the Church doctrine on his life and sufferings; the other will have nothing to do with an interpretation of this kind. Both interpretations, like a great many others that have been made of these old writers, being very wide of the mark, as I think, because neglecting the point of view of the men who penned the words, starting with inadequate and sometimes wholly erroneous ideas of the writers' intentions, and with nothing like accurate acquaintance with their feelings. These men were men with great literary capacity. Like the greatest of the men of this class, they were most amenable to the influences of their time, played upon by every circumstance in the life around them, lifted up beyond measure by the joy of it, saddened beyond expression by the sorrow of it. They were the true spokesmen of their countrymen and contemporaries, the soul and heart of their age: genuinely human, as human as Browning, Carlyle or Ruskin: poets in the very first degree—religious men above all things. And it strikes me more and more that all the greatest have been great in proportion to the religious strain in their character—religious, I mean, of course, in the way that I explain to you now and again, in their intense moral earnestness. I might read you off a list of names that would make this clear, from the sages and literary monarchs and powers in India, China, Persia, Greece, to the really creative minds among ourselves and on the continent. In my study of the great German, for instance, nothing has more impressed me than his deep and true religiousness, and the early evidence of this vein in his character—his genuine appreciation of our Bible men and histories, and the powerful hold they took of his imagination—the deep channel which this whole current of life has plainly cut in his soul. Although ostensibly a literary man—poet and novelist and song-writer and dramatist—I could bring from his works better interpretations of our sacred literature, and more correct principles of interpretation, than from those of any professed Biblical critic. I could also gather from the same source hints for a philosophy of religion that are not to be obtained in any professed treatise on the subject. And no book on religious experience, as known to a pure and simple and earnest soul, can furnish matter so near to what is best in our Gospels as his "Wilhelm Meister."

Our Old Testament men, I was saying, were poets and religious in the highest degree—human—historical,—and to be understood only as we come to them and meet them on this ground. I am not anxious even that you should approach them as thinking them inspired. They were inspired in a very true sense—in a sense that I trust we shall be able to reverence, and understand better than we have done. I am anxious that you should come near them and listen to them, not as to men speaking theology, as it is called—not as to men forewriting doctrine and foretelling actual and individual fact. With notions like these in our heads, we shall never get near the men nor their thoughts. What they wrote, they wrote out of the fulness of their hearts. The deep experiences of great natures are in their words. They were not building up theories, but giving out facts; and to pass over such a passage as this with the thought in our minds only, that here we have a mysterious prefigurement of Christ—or with the opposing thought, that we have nothing of the kind, is the very way to misunderstand our best literature, and to allow the most choice truths to slip through our fingers. I may set your minds at rest at once by saying, that the prophet is not speaking of Jesus; but that is because he is giving voice to a truth that takes in Jesus and every life upon this earth which in its main feature resembles his. The Church has been thus far correct in seeing Christ's life in these words, but quite wrong in limiting them to that; and in so limiting them has done great injustice to the Hebrew author, and kept us in the dark, so far, as to his real meaning and the greatness of his thought. And there is, in fact, the most solid truth in the doctrine which has been built up with help from the material that this great mind has supplied—very much, as I am inclined to think, through the material so supplied—I mean the doctrine, as we know it, under the name of vicarious suffering. Here again, as with the human experiences of this prophet, men start off in two directions. Some will hear of vicarious suffering only in connection with Christ; others will hear of no such a thing as vicarious suffering at all—missing again an unquestionable fact in history, a fact borne witness to by men who had no sympathy with the theological way of putting things, but who, like Isaiah, had seen, and in their own lives had felt, the only truth that lies in an expression of this kind. I shall give you the truth in modern words—in the words also of a poet, as it chances, and, like the Hebrew poet, a great and earnest and religious poet: "Live with thy century, but be not its creature; produce for your contemporaries, but what they need, not what they praise. Without having shared its guilt, share with nobler resignation its punishment; and bear thyself with freedom under the yoke, which they equally badly do without and bear. Through the firm courage with which thou rejectest their happiness, thou wilt prove to them that thy cowardice is not subjected to their sufferings." That is a long way behind the perception and the picture of Isaiah, but gives perhaps, in language more familiar to us, what the Hebrew poet meant; and these words of the great and good Schiller, true artist and poet and teacher of men, have been for years my commentary on vicarious suffering, and my gloss to the fifty-third chapter of Isaiah. And while I am at it, I may as well give you the experiences of his friend and fellow-labourer Goethe—words which are tenderer and less stern than the rigorous Schiller could utter, entering more fully than even Isaiah ventures to do, into the difficulties and trials of a true servant and teacher and vicarious sufferer. This next quotation is concerned with the servant of God as an artist, and I am rather glad that it is so, for it will help to make us familiar with the truth, that it is not in one way only, nor in one line of business and pursuit, that we can do this service to God and be called upon to make the sacrifice for men—not in one, but in all the lines of business and activity which men honestly follow after. The observation which I am to quote to you, arose out of a remark that excellent works of art were very rare in recent times; on which it is said: "It cannot be easily imagined nor seen what circumstances must do for the artist; and then in the case of the greatest genius—the most decided talent, the demands which he has continually to make on himself are infinite—the diligence which is necessary for his upbuilding, unspeakable." That, I may say, is not a common opinion. We suppose great natural gifts to mean great ease and excuse for infinite indulgence. The men who have them can come, without effort, so swiftly at what other men toil after. But we forget that greatness is not satisfied with coming to what other men toil after—that to come at its mark, it must not only have gifts above others, but work more severely than the lowest hireling. The upbuilding and finishing of a great nature is not to be done, and never has been done, unless in the way here noticed. However, to continue this quotation: "If mere circumstances do little for him"—your genius and servant are subject, like the meanest, to circumstances—"if he observes that the world is easy to satisfy, and longs for an easy, pleasant, comfortable make-believe, would it be surprising if indulgence and love of self held him fast to what was commonplace? It would be odd," says this man of the world, "if he would not barter for current wares, money and praise, rather than choose the right way, which would lead him more or less towards a miserable martyrdom." I have been thus particular in giving you these illustrations of the Hebrew prophet's principle, because you will more readily see, in this modern way of setting it, what an important and universal law of life there is in it, and in the doctrine also which has been too narrowly built upon it. But I think that neither Schiller nor Goethe has gone so deeply into the true servant's experiences, into the magnanimous but mild surrender of himself, into the power and gentleness of the soul that is content to be wounded for the healing of others—to make himself acquainted with grief and sorrow that are not his own—to bear with infinite meekness and patience the evils and calamities of which his own spirit is clear; there is nothing in these modern instances of this ancient depth of insight. Schiller's servant is faithful, but with a certain pride, and haughtiness, and scorn—a feeling of supremacy. Goethe's servant—the poor, struggling and fallen one we are all familiar with—cannot wait for the travail of his soul, but satisfies it grossly with immediate reward. And these two kinds of the servant are common enough; the typical one of the great Hebrew poet, most rare, beautiful and, as it seems to us, unapproachable. One cannot wonder that men, looking for a living example, have with something like unanimity discerned the only approach to it in the Lamb of Calvary—in him who lived among his fellows "as one that serveth"—who gave men, not what they liked, but what was good for them, but gave it with grace and infinite persuasiveness—who allowed no seducement to divert him from his purpose, but followed it even when he saw the "miserable martyrdom" it was leading him to—following it, not boastfully, but with innocence and uncomplaining modesty. We must all see the likeness, the aptness of every line of the description. It might stand as heading to the Gospels, and would be the fittest inscription over the Cross. The meaning of that teaching, of that sorrow, of that death—of such utter and overwhelming disaster and grief and vexation, associated with a life and character that we can find no match to—is, if you will look at it closely, set out to us by this gifted seer—going out into mystery, but not into a mystery that is repugnant to our thoughts, but to one only that rises above the level of our moral life—traced for us in the most human characters —level with our deepest sympathies—true, most strictly true, to the best known facts in the best of all lives:—the meaning of this being, that the best and the noblest of our kind are not exempt from the sorrows and sufferings and sins of their fellows—not exempt from them, nay, more— that the highest in worth feels these evils the keenest, and, if there is overthrow, he is the first to be overthrown. There is such unity in our race, and it comes out so strongly in our strongest and our greatest, that they are weighted with the evils and weaknesses of the weakest. The Cross and the Man on it have been often spoken of as a solace to mankind; we can all in our trials and sorrows and struggles, it is said, find a companion in this Man of sorrow and travail. And there is great truth in the soothing power of companionship like this where it is inwardly realized. But the Cross speaks to us of something more than this. Great as this lesson is, it has a greater and a grander. Our bitterest griefs are personal, our sorrows individual; and the Cross, although the symbol of grief meekly and nobly borne, and a thought strengthening to every burdened spirit, rises into a higher region of life, and holds forth to the world something more divine than sympathy with personal suffering. It is the sign of the true and faithful servant of Isaiah, the ideal teacher of Schiller, the tempted but victorious artist of Goethe. It gives in picture what Christian thought has struggled to express, and has only faintly and feebly stammered out—stammerings that we later men have not altogether been just to, but stammerings which we have shown no ability as yet to make more coherent, because our lives have not been travelling in the direction of this thought, but in an opposite direction. And what is the truth in these servants', teachers', artists' lives—the virtual conception beneath the somewhat arid phraseology of religious thought—the human and universal, if at present morally a little incomprehensible to us, note in Christ's life? Not, surely, what a somewhat mechanical and unpoetical intelligence has made of it. Nor yet what a narrow and lynx-eyed criticism describes. Neither of these. But what great moral and intellectual natures have felt to be the law of their lives—that the great and the good are not lords in the earth, but servants; that their goodness does not free them from the evils and pains which are the direct consequences of sin and wrong; but that, on the contrary, as Schiller has it, being free from the sin, they must yet share its punishment; being the more punished, the more free they are from the sin—bruised for sins not his own—wounded for transgressions of which he was entirely innocent—led to a miserable martyrdom (I quote my modern expositor) to atone for what his soul detested. I am giving you no theory, my friends. No theory that I know at present would quite contain this very certain historical truth. I am giving you a truth as it was seen by a good and earnest man in a great national emergency in his own country, and which he set forth in the only style that, so far as I can see, such a truth can be laid out, in poetry and symbol, which might duly reproduce the historical facts.

We have quite other notions of goodness and greatness, notions something like those of the Gentiles that Christ spoke about. We imagine their possessors to be lifted clear of all calamities—to be what we term a law to themselves—not one with the multitude, but, from their supremacy and endowments of heart and intellect, infinitely removed into some serene and undisturbed region of life and thought. Look over your histories again, my friends. No great man ever lived at this elevation. The greatest could never tolerate the acceptance of service. They have been ever forward in rendering it. They never could live withdrawn from the evils that have come, and must come in the wake of wrongs—but are to be found, as a matter of fact and history, in the very breach, exposed to the very fiercest of the fire. And, if it comes to reckoning of wounds, find, if you can, a spot in them that is not pierced. The law of virtue evidently is not happiness, in the sense of immunity from suffering. My text is a memorial of great national virtue and true and noble patriotism, rewarded as you see —not by being safely protected from what properly and naturally and justly came upon a weak and demoralized and sinful people. The foremost men among them in loyalty to truth and goodness and right, are undermost in the overthrow. None bruised like them: none stricken to the soul like them: none put to grief like them. So deep is the feeling of community of life in the soul of the man who has been awakened to goodness. And it is not a feeling of community—there is actual community, as I am going to show. They cannot separate themselves from their fellows. They must bear their burdens, an' they should sink beneath them—take home their sorrows, an' the heart should break. "Let the cup pass!"—a thing impossible until he become untrue to himself and completely invert his life. Sad picture of virtue and of worth, it is said—sickly, unreal—giving no hope—a joyless thing—taking the sunshine from goodness, and the beauty from a pure humanity. Most of us would like to see a much clearer separation between good and bad than such thoughts suggest. We prefer to think of the good coming out scatheless. Isaiah does not teach this kind of philosophy, and no instructor of any genius has taught a lesson resembling that. The full force of a woe in which they have no hand must fall upon the servants' heads. It may spend much of its force upon their heads, and come more gently upon the less worthy and more strictly responsible. Men who merely look on cry out on the injustice and unequalness of such a fate; but you never heard—and this is worth remembering—one of these servants utter a complaint. "As a sheep before her shearers," he yields himself to the divineness of the law that links him to his fellows, inseparably yokes him to their evils and their consequences—his heart, which had been enlarged for goodness and love, crammed full with grief and sorrow—his soul, become a fair expanse for beauty and goodness, has its fair dimensions filled with woes—his virtue grown strong to take up burdens that belong to others. The realization—terrible to us and altogether mysterious as we are at present constituted—of a vain sentiment we speak often about and imagine we admire and understand—that God has made us of one blood with our fellows, that they are our brothers, knit to us indissolubly—that we are so bound to them, that their misery, their wrongs, their evil, fall upon us, and fall with force the more tremendous, the more clear we have kept our souls from wrong. Bound to them too—and this is the other and cheering side—so that the life that is in the servant, the virtue and the love, the goodness and the worth, can flow from him to his fellows. If there is a passage of misery in this human unity of life, passage of misery from the many to the one, there is passage of healing from the one to the many. If he is involved with them in the very strictest reality, and the most human and natural way, in their evils and results, they are involved with him also, in no mechanical and unreal fashion, in his goodness and its consequences. If he lies stricken with them, the most stricken of all, through the power that makes him thus their fellow-sufferer and intimate in grief, he is made their healer and life-giver. It is not sympathy I am speaking of, my friends; it is oneness of life. The servant is one with all—the sickness that has fallen upon all comes upon him, as one with them, organically part of all; and the power of health that is in him is not restricted to him, but must flow freely through every part of the organism, gradually lifting them out of their misery, slowly raising them to the vigour and robustness and beauty of life that is in the servant himself. You have heard of the solidarity of the human race; it is a favourite phrase with many just now. The true servant is the man who speaks little of this, but who, in many ages and various countries, has felt himself one with all, sickening with their illnesses, and from the fountain of his life infusing them with the sap of his own soul. And by his power to suffer, and by his actual bearing of sins and sorrows that were not his own, can we estimate his power to heal, and raise, and bless. The deeper his bruises, the more radical the world's healing; his capacity to share our griefs is the measure of his power to give the world the joy of his life. If he is so one with man that he can bear the world's sins, he can remove these sins; the darkness he experienced is the measure of the light he can impart; and if his soul, in the teaching of the Church, could descend to hell, that is for us the best evidence that he can lift men to true blessedness.

www.ingramcontent.com/pod-product-compliance
Lightning Source LLC
Chambersburg PA
CBHW030258170426
43202CB00009B/790